Images of War
Auschwitz
Death Camp

Ian Baxter

Pen & Sword
MILITARY

First published in Great Britain in 2009 and Reprinted in 2010 by
PEN & SWORD MILITARY
an imprint of
Pen & Sword Books Ltd,
47 Church Street,
Barnsley,
South Yorkshire.
S70 2AS

A CIP record for this book is available from the British Library.

ISBN 978 1 84884 072 0

Printed and bound by CPI UK

Pen & Sword Books Ltd incorporates the Imprints of
Pen & Sword Aviation, Pen & Sword Maritime,
Pen & Sword Military, Wharncliffe Local History, Pen & Sword Select,
Pen & Sword Military Classics and Leo Cooper.

For a complete list of Pen & Sword titles please contact
Pen & Sword Books Limited
47 Church Street, Barnsley, South Yorkshire, S70 2AS, England
E-mail: enquiries@pen-and-sword.co.uk
Website: www.pen-and-sword.co.uk

Contents

Introduction

The concentration camp at Auschwitz-Birkenau was the location of the single largest mass murder in history. Over one million men, women, and children were brought to this death camp and murdered in the gas chambers. Others, however, died a more slow painful death as the ravages of disease and starvation took a hold.

Auschwitz Death Camp, is a chilling highly illustrated record of those that were sent to the camp to work and be murdered. It chronicles those that actually run the camp and vividly describes in detail using some 250 photographs together with detailed captions and accompanying text, how Auschwitz evolved from a brutal labour camp at the beginning of the war, to a factory of death.

Each chapter gives a highly accurate portrait of how people lived, worked and died in the Auschwitz Death Camp. It describes the men who conceived, created, and constructed the killing facility, and how the camp became the centrepiece for a vast labour pool for various industrial complexes erected around Auschwitz.

Auschwitz Death Camp provides a unique insight into a camp where over sixty-three-years ago was separated from the outside world. Only through illustrated records will the reader realize the magnitude of horror that was inflicted on innocent men, women and children.

The Author

Ian Baxter is a military historian who specialises in German Twentieth Century military history. He has written more than twenty books including *'Wolf' Hitler's Wartime Headquarters, Poland – The Eighteen Day Victory March, Panzers In North Africa, The Ardennes Offensive, The Western Campaign, The 12th SS Panzer-Division Hitlerjugend, The Waffen-SS on the Western Front, The Waffen-SS on the Eastern Front, The Red Army At Stalingrad, Elite German Forces of World War II, Armoured Warfare, German Tanks of War, Blitzkrieg, Panzer-Divisions At War, Hitler's Panzers, German Armoured Vehicles of World War Two, Last Two Years of the Waffen-SS At War, German Soldier Uniforms and Insignia, German Guns of the Third Reich, Defeat to Retreat: The Last Years of the German Army At War 1943 – 1945, Operation Bagration – the destruction of Army Group Centre, German Guns of the Third Reich, Rommel and the Afrika Korps, the Sixth Army and the Road to Stalingrad, U-Boat War,* and most recently, *Hitler's Eastern Front Headquarters 'Wolf's Lair' 1941 – 1945.* He has written over one hundred journals including *Last days of Hitler, Wolf's Lair, Story of the V1 and V2 rocket programme, Secret Aircraft of World War Two, Rommel At Tobruk, Hitler's War With His Generals, Secret British Plans To Assassinate Hitler, SS At Arnhem, Hitlerjugend, Battle Of Caen 1944, Gebirgsjäger At War, Panzer Crews, Hitlerjugend Guerrillas, Last Battles in the East, Battle of Berlin,* and many more. He has also reviewed numerous military studies for publication, supplied thousands of photographs and important documents to various publishers and film production companies worldwide, and lectures to various schools, colleges and universities throughout the United Kingdom and Southern Ireland.

Acknowledgments

It is with the greatest pleasure that I use this opportunity on concluding this book to thank those who helped make this volume possible. My expression of gratitude first goes to Wojciech P∏osa,

Head of the Auschwitz-Birkenau State Archive, who gave generously his time whilst I sifted through many hundreds of images at the Auschwitz museum during a number of visits between 2006 and 2008.

I wish to also thank the staff of the United States Holocaust Museum. The archive has been an unfailing source; supplying me with a number of photographs that were obtained from numerous sources, including obtaining images from a rare SS photograph album of the Nazi leadership at Auschwitz. This 1944 album belonged to and was created by *SS-Obersturmführer* Karl Höcker, the adjutant to the commandant of Auschwitz, *SS-Sturmbannführer* Richard Baer. Höcker was stationed at Auschwitz from May 1944 until the evacuation of the camp in January 1945. The photographs show Höcker with other SS officers in Auschwitz in the summer and autumn of 1944, and provide the reader with a new understanding of their lives and activities of the camp. Other images supplied by the United States Holocaust Museum include a photograph album known as the 'Auschwitz album'. The original owner of the album, was Lili Jacob (later Zelmanovic Meier), who was deported with her family to Auschwitz in late May 1944 from Bilke (today: Bil'ki, Ukraine), a small town near Berehovo in Transcarpathian Rus which was then part of Hungary. They arrived on May 26, 1944, the same day that professional SS photographers photographed the arrival of the train and the selection process. After surviving Auschwitz, forced labour in Morchenstern, a Gross-Rosen subcamp, and transfer to Dora-Mittelbau where she was liberated, Lili Jacob discovered an album containing the 'Auschwitz photographs' in a drawer of a bedside table in an abandoned SS barracks while she was recovering from typhus. After the war she brought the original album with her when she immigrated to the United States, and these images were used as part evidence at the Frankfurt Auschwitz Trial (in which Lili Jacob testified and in which Karl Höcker was a defendant). In 1983, Lili Jacob donated the album of photographs of her transport's arrival in Auschwitz to the Yad Vashem Museum.

I wish also to thank my friends Chandran Sivanson and Kevin Bowden for spending time with me whilst researching at Auschwitz. A very warm thank you to Chandran for providing some of the images for this book, one of which appears on the front cover.

Chapter One
Evolution of Auschwitz

The town of Auschwitz (Oswiecim) was situated in a remote corner of south-western Poland, in a marshy valley where the Sola River flows into the Vistula about thirty-five miles west of the ancient city of Krakow. The town was virtually unknown outside Poland and following the occupation of the country Oswiecim was incorporated into the *Reich* together with Upper Silesia and renamed by the German authorities as Auschwitz. Prior to the war, the town's population was 12,000, including nearly 5,000 Jews. The surrounding countryside in the foothills of the Tatra Mountains, whose peaks remained covered in snow all year round, lies in a humid often foggy swampy valley. During the winter the weather is harsh and the whole area could often lie in snow until late March, or even early April. During the spring the whole area would be revived and could look very beautiful, especially when the warmer weather produced a mixture of wild flowers through the sprawling meadows.

It was here in the small district town of Auschwitz that the Germans had chosen a site for a new concentration camp. Originally it had been a former Polish labour exchange and artillery barracks. The location for the site was deemed well situated for Auschwitz had very good railway connections and was isolated from outside observation.

After visiting the site on 27 April 1940, *SS-Hauptsturmführer* Rudolf Höss received approval to go ahead and commence construction and adapt the new site at Auschwitz. It was also agreed that it would house around 10,000 prisoners. A few days later on 4 May 1940, Höss was officially named as commandant of the new Auschwitz quarantine camp.

In order to construct and transform the new camp and adapt the twenty brick barracks for the inmates Höss had been given a construction budget

1. A retouched colour photograph taken of the thirty-six-year-old Rudolf Höss holding the rank of *SS-Hauptsturmführer* in 1936 during his posting at Dachau. Höss became commandant of Auschwitz in May 1940. [Courtesy of the Auschwitz-Birkenau Museum – colour enhancement Richard Markey]

1a. Construction of Auschwitz. I in the winter of 1940. Prisoners digging foundations of heating or plumbing pipes near the main reception building (Aufnahmegebäude) in Auschwitz I. [Courtesy of the Auschwitz-Birkenau Museum]

of two million *Reich Marks*. With this generous allowance he would be given the task of cleaning the existing barracks for the guards, rebuilding the two barracks outside the fence into officers' quarters and a hospital for the garrison, build a barrack for the *Blockführer* at the gate, construct eight guard towers around the perimeter of the camp, build a hayloft, install a crematorium in the abandoned powder magazine building, and tidy the three-storey house on the edge of the existing camp in order to make it habitable for him and his family.

During May and early June construction of the camp progressed relatively slowly, but a fence with second-hand barbed wire was soon being installed around the perimeter of the camp, and new buildings began to be constructed. At the entrance of Auschwitz Höss had a new steel gate forged in a hurriedly built workshop and a frame built. Blazoned along the top of the gates frame he had the inscription erected that he liked so much at Dachau, *'Arbeit Macht Frei'* - Work Makes You Free. For him the words marked a new journey for all prisoners that passed through these gates, and through hard labour he believed would somehow bring the prisoners a spiritual freedom.

Throughout July and early August work continued on the camp. The labour force lived and worked in appalling conditions. By October there were a mixture of inmates that consisted of Jews, members of the intelligentsia, resistance and political prisoners, together with Polish Catholic priests. All of them were struggling for survival, and yet nothing was done to alleviate the dire conditions. Under equipped, lacking protective gear, and malnourished, the inmates went about their place of work constantly being mentally and physically abused by the guards.

By early December work had considerably forged ahead in spite of the considerable harsh weather conditions imposed on the work force. The whole site, when completed, was to have a very large camp kitchen, utility, theatre, registration buildings, *Blockführer* officer, commandant's office, camp administration offices, SS hospital, a fully operational crematorium, Gestapo offices, medical block, and a large water pool

2. Showing the infamous gates of 'Arbeit Macht Frei', work makes you free. The commandant of Auschwitz firmly believed that inmates gained a sense of discipline by working during their imprisonment, and this discipline would enable them to withstand the harsh environment of prison life. He believed that endless labour brought about a kind of spiritual freedom. The inscription was the work of a Polish political prisoner called Jan Liwacz. Jan was a professional artsmith and had arrived at Auschwitz in the second transport sent from Wisnicz Prison on 20 June 1940. It still stands today as a reminder. [Courtesy of the HITM ARCHIVE & Auschwitz-Birkenau Museum]

3. The commandant Rudolf Höss's former family residence as it stands today. Right of the house is the garden, whilst on the left is the private entrance used by Höss. The commandant's offices can just be seen behind a tree and row of conifers. [Courtesy of the HITM ARCHIVE & Auschwitz-Birkenau Museum]

4. A photograph taken from inside the garden of the commandant's former residence, known as the Höss villa. It was an imposing two-storey stucco building situated in the north-eastern corner of the camp. On this side of the building the house was reached by a concrete path and a flight of concrete steps leading to the side door with a porch, and overlooked the garden. The garden itself was predominantly situated to the side of the house and consisted of a number of trees and shrubberies from the previous occupants. A fence with barbed wire was erected around the perimeter of the garden and the house, in order to divide it from the main camp. In November 1940, a new high concrete fencing was constructed and topped with barbed wire to replace the old fencing around the entire boundary of the camp. The new fencing was also installed at the rear and the sides of the Höss villa, making the house completely separated from the camp and virtually invisible from the garden, except for the roofs and chimneys of the Commandant's Office and Administration buildings. The fence to the rear of the house, which hid the Commandant's Office, Administration offices, SS guardhouse and the newly constructed crematorium, was further hidden by a large mound of earth placed behind the fence, and trees planted. Höss had been particularly insistent on trying to conceal the villa from the camp as much as possible, and made it known that he wanted his family to live in absolute privacy. [Courtesy of the HITM ARCHIVE & Auschwitz-Birkenau Museum]

reserve for fire emergencies. It was also intended to have twenty-two two-storey buildings converted into prisoner quarters. Plans were drafted and approved for a prisoner hospital and offices and quarters for some of the camp's prisoners. The majority of these buildings were constructed in red-brick and run in straight rows

5. A photograph taken from the perimeter of Auschwitz.I on the Rajsko to Auschwitz road looking towards the commandant's office, camp administration office and the SS hospital. Each morning Rudolf Höss would walk across to Department I, the commandant's office, and would converse with his office secretaries, answer any urgent messages or telegrams and issue his daily written orders to his subordinates. The letters, telegrams, various telephone call messages and other paper work that were classed not as urgent were regularly taken home to be dealt with in his study. [Courtesy of the HITM ARCHIVE & Auschwitz-Birkenau Museum]

6. One of a number of signs posted around the camp warning prisoners not to pass beyond the sign into a prohibited stretch of land bordering the high tension electric fence. The red brick building in front of the fence is the registration building. Here new prisoners would be catalogued, receive their camp registration number, have their photograph taken, before being escorted by armed guard through the main gates to serve their sentence. [Courtesy of the HITM ARCHIVE & Auschwitz-Birkenau Museum]

throughout the camp and were given block numbers for identification purposes. The *Blockführer*'s guardhouse, however, was a wooden structure and this was built just outside the main gate. Another building under construction outside the main perimeter was a very large red-brick building, known as the registration building. Here new prisoners would be catalogued, receive their camp registration number, have their photograph taken, before being escorted by armed guard through the main gates to serve their sentence.

Most of the buildings that were built at Auschwitz and those planned for the future served merely to house and provide the basic needs for the prisoners, guards and SS staff that run the camp. But there was one building constructed that symbolized the camp's culture, this was known as Block 13 and by 1941 re-numbered Block 11. The building looked like any other red-brick building that housed prisoners. But it had not been built to serve a unique purpose. It had been chosen by the Political Department or Gestapo to be used purely for interrogating and torturing inmates with a variety of

7. A photograph taken looking down towards the prisoners' quarters, Block 25. On the right of the electric fence is the former registration building, and on the left is the camp kitchen. Note two of the camp's prefabricated guard towers on the right. These were erected in early 1941. The whole site, when completed, was to have a very large camp kitchen, utility, theatre, registration buildings, *Blockführer* officer, commandant's office, camp administration offices, SS hospital, a fully operational crematorium, Gestapo offices, medical block, and a large water pool reserve for fire emergencies. [Courtesy of the HITM ARCHIVE & Auschwitz-Birkenau Museum]

brutal and terrifying methods. In order to hold the prisoners for questioning prison cells had been specially constructed in the basement. One of the most notorious of the camp personnel that ran the block was *SS-Untersturmführer* Max Grabner. It was Grabner who decided the fate of the prisoners held at Block 13. Those unfortunate enough to be sentenced to death were first taken to the washrooms on the ground

8. Prisoner block houses in Auschwitz. I. The building on the left is Block 24. It was here in the summer of 1943 that Höss was requested to create a brothel for the prisoners. SS-Reichsführer Heinrich Himmler had decided that providing brothels across the concentration camp system would increase productivity by offering all non-Jewish hard working prisoners an incentive to worker harder. [Courtesy of the HITM ARCHIVE & Auschwitz-Birkenau Museum]

9. Looking down towards the concrete perimeter fence. On the left is prisoner Block 14 and Block 3. On the right is prisoner Block15 and Block 4. Initially when the camp first opened in mid-1940, it was intended to have twenty-two two-storey buildings converted into prisoner quarters. Plans were drafted and approved for a prisoner hospital and offices and quarters for some of the camp's prisoners. The majority of these buildings were constructed in red-brick and run in straight rows throughout the camp and were given block numbers for identification purposes. [Courtesy of the HITM ARCHIVE & Auschwitz-Birkenau Museum]

floor and ordered to strip naked. They were then hastily escorted out into a secluded courtyard and shot against a brick wall.

* * * * * * * *

Early 1941 began with a series of important deliberations for the SS as Auschwitz begun to slowly enter a new crucial stage of its evolution. During Himmler's visit to the camp on 1 March the *Reichsführer* outlined new grandiose plans for the area. Just outside the town of Auschwitz Himmler, Höss with a delegation of other SS officials arrived in a marshy tract of land in the Auschwitz district of Zasole, adjacent to the parent camp. Accompanied with maps and various architectural drawings of the land Himmler announced that the area they were standing on had been chosen as a new potential site. Auschwitz, he exclaimed, would be soon expanded, and there would be a huge satellite camp constructed far greater than anything else planned or envisaged. This new camp, he said, would house a population of at least 100,000 prisoners.

Himmler not only proposed to establish a huge satellite camp, but also intended to increase the Auschwitz camp population from the anticipated 10,000 inmates, to a staggering 30,000. He made it clear to Höss that the massive increase in prisoner population was urgently required for labour availability, which was key to the progressive development of the region. The *Reichsführer* envisaged that gangs of slave labour would be used to improve the dikes along the Sola and Vistula, and would also be put to work demolishing sites in the town for new building developments that were planned. In order to undertake these new building developments, he said, all Jewish and Polish residents living around the camp were to be evicted and incarcerated in a camp in the neighbourhood of Auschwitz, and used as unskilled construction workers. By evicting these people it would allow the town to be available for the factory staff of a new massive enterprise that Himmler was eager to see built in the local area – I.G. Farben.

For sometime I.G. Farben had shown interest in the region around Auschwitz, and particularly welcomed using large numbers of skilled and unskilled construction workers from the concentration camps. It was estimated that between 8,000 and 12,000 men would be required to construct the factory, and with the *Reichsführer*'s new plans to increase the pool of prisoners at Auschwitz to 30,000, he had more than enough. By expanding Auschwitz he not only provided I.G. Farben with adequate amounts of slave labour, but could commit 10,000 inmates to his planned agricultural estate as well.

The *Reichsführer*'s audacious plans of turning Auschwitz into a huge agricultural experimental centre was still very much a fundamental part in his overall vision. He also made it known he had no intention of giving up the plans for the gravel and sand pit enterprises either. He tried his best to assure Höss that the enterprises would be good for the region, and it could not be made possible without expanding and developing Auschwitz. It was for this reason, he said, I.G. Farben had to be given the highest priority. A site had already been chosen for a factory about two miles away. It would be built to produce synthetic rubber, called Buna, and inmates from Auschwitz were to help construct it. Other construction workers too from Germany would be brought in and be accommodated in vacant homes in Auschwitz town. The town itself would be redeveloped and schools and hospitals built purely for the German workers.

10. On the left is prisoner Block 1, 12 and 22. On the right between the high tension electric fence is the commandant's office, camp administration offices and the SS hospital. In 1940, most of the buildings that were built at Auschwitz and those planned for the future served merely to house and provide the basic needs for the prisoners, guards and SS staff that run the camp. [Courtesy of the HITM ARCHIVE & Auschwitz-Birkenau Museum]

11. A photograph of the former commandant's office, Rudolf Höss, at Auschwitz. I. This large, imposing building generally handled matters concerning SS staff. All records, weapons and other important military equipment were stored here. Transport and communication matters were also controlled from this headquarters. The office was divided into a number of different sections: office supplies, communications office, judicial affairs, weapons, military supplies, and the engineer's office. Höss had his own personal office, as well as a boardroom where he and his staff gathered twice a week. [Courtesy of the HITM ARCHIVE & Auschwitz-Birkenau Museum]

Himmler also announced to Höss that he intended to move some of the arms industry into the area as well.

Whilst plans for the expansion of Auschwitz evolved during the summer of 1941, living conditions there were appalling for the prisoners. A great many of the inmates were looking increasingly emaciated, and the prison hospital was filling-up daily with the sick. Though those Poles incapacitated by illness and disease could be replaced, the authorities were becoming progressively more insistent on removing those unfit for work, and having them executed. Executions at the camp had increased immeasurably by middle of 1941. On almost a daily basis messages would arrive direct from the Security Police, or from the RSHA in Berlin, stating which prisoners should be shot or hanged. Every four to six weeks the Katowitz military court would visit the camp and the accused prisoners, most of which were already inmates, were brought before a tribunal, and in many cases were sentenced to death. The extent of the executions had in fact increased to such high numbers that the Gestapo decided it would be more efficient to bring the condemned straight to the crematorium, where they were ordered to undress in the mortuary before being shot. Their naked corpses were then incinerated in the room next door and the ashes disposed with the rest of the day's killings.

Since September 1940, the Auschwitz crematorium had been working at a steady pace burning the bodies of prisoners that died of natural death or were killed or executed. By 1941, the crematorium had in fact reached its maximum capacity of eighteen bodies per hour. In direct response to the dramatic increase of deaths in the camp Höss was prompted to authorise the expansion of the crematorium. After all he was well aware why it was most important to equip and expand his camp with a facility to murder, for the destruction of Bolshevism was about to begin in earnest.

Although Auschwitz remained a camp primarily for Polish prisoners, Höss received reports that the SS were actually weeding out commissars that were found hiding in German army POW camps. The first of these Soviet prisoners were transported to Auschwitz in July. Several hundred of them were marched through the main gate, and from the moment they arrived they were treated much worse than the Polish inmates. They were hated at Auschwitz. Many of them were beaten and tortured, whilst some were shot in the gravel pits or were condemned to the cellars of Block 11. Here they were locked in the dark cold cells and left to starve to death.

As a result of these increased deaths at Auschwitz the crematorium was once again working to full capacity. Executions were now so frequent that Höss was compelled to discuss at his meetings a more effective method of killing than just starving, shooting and hanging the victims, or having them murdered by lethal injection. Höss told his staff that to find an effective method was essential to guarantee the rapid effectiveness of cleansing the camp of what he deemed were undesirables, and those unfit for work.

In late August *SS Obersturmbannführer* Adolf Eichmann of the RSHA in Berlin arrived at Auschwitz to meet with the commandant. Eichmann was a Jewish emigration specialist who had been given the task of facilitating and managing the logistics of mass deportations of Jews to ghettos and concentration camps in Nazi-occupied Eastern Europe. Apart from discussing plans to start transporting Jews to Auschwitz another important question on Eichmann's list was the design of an improved killing facility at the camp, which would be capable of exterminating larger numbers of inmates. Those that were regarded subhuman for instance like Russian POWs were certainly on the agenda for liquidation, and it was suggested that it would be practical to use the Russian POWs in a killing experiment.

It was agreed that carbon monoxide chambers used in the mobile gas chamber vans were far too expensive. Instead, Höss proposed using hydro cyanide. He told Eichmann that he was in the process of constructing a delousing installation at Auschwitz and could perhaps use a lethal substance made up of hydro cyanide. The idea appealed greatly to Eichmann, and Höss informed him that he would instruct his deputy, Fritzsch, who was in charge of the fumigation and the disinfection process of the camp, to experiment.

On 1 September, just before Höss left Auschwitz on business, he told Fritzsch that he had been given the dutiful task of gassing Russian POWs, and should carry out a pilot experiment with the chemicals used for delousing. In his view, if they killed infestations of insects, it was possible they could kill human pests as well. This order has come from Berlin, he said, and we must ensure its secrecy. Fritzsch eager to impress his superiors willingly agreed and told his commandant that he would undertake a pilot experiment without delay.

On 3 September the SS conducted the first mass execution using crystallized prussic acid, which was sold in tins marked under the name of Zyklon B. Fritzsch had chosen the basement of Block 11. First he ensured that the windows and other areas of the basement were made airtight before removing the condemned out from there sickbeds and hovels. During the cover of darkness they were escorted down to Block 11 where they were herded tightly into the underground cells. Fritzsch then threw the Zyklon B crystals into the room where Russian prisoners with the sick inmates were standing. Although many of them were asphyxiated within twenty minutes of the gassing, some prisoners did in fact survive the ordeal, and had to be shot.

12. At Auschwitz I. a sign reads 'Beware High Tension Electric Fence, Danger to Life'. On the right are prisoner block houses. [Courtesy of the HITM ARCHIVE & Auschwitz-Birkenau Museum]

It was agreed that the basement was not ideal and that they find an alternative method of dropping the Zyklon B into a gas chamber. Fritzsch mentioned the camp's crematorium was the most suitable location for a killing facility. It not only had a flat roof, but could easily be adapted with various openings in order to allow the Zyklon B crystals to be poured through. The new powerful ventilation system that had just been fitted in the morgue would be more than capable of dealing with the poisonous gas.

Once the crematorium had been prepared for a mass killing experiment 900 Russian soldiers were chosen to be gassed. The gassing of the Soviet soldiers took place on 16 September, and it was a complete success. No longer would the SS have

13. A photograph taken between the double fence perimeter between the camp administration offices and prisoner block no.12. At the far end is one of the camp's prefabricated wooden guard towers. [Courtesy of the HITM ARCHIVE & Auschwitz-Birkenau Museum]

to look into the eyes of their victims as they murdered them. Now they could transport their victims straight into a specially adapted gas chamber and have them killed altogether, sparing, as Höss called, a bloodbath. This new procedure appealed greatly to the SS. They had found by simple innovation that the new arrivals could quite easily be led into the crematorium not knowing they were going to be killed, simply disinfected by taking a shower. It had proven very easy to get the inmates into the gas chamber by deception rather than using varying degrees of force. By using gas as a method of execution Höss saw its implementation less stressful for the guards that were assigned to these new murderous duties.

Whilst the improved killing facility at Auschwitz had more or less been achieved with the use of Zyklon B crystals, Rudolf Höss had become increasingly concerned at the amount of Russian POWs that would be sent to the camp and pass through the crematorium. By September the Germans had already captured an estimated three million Soviet prisoners. Some 100,000 of them were transferred from the Army to the SS in September, and many were earmarked for Auschwitz. According to a report, Himmler had ordered Hans Kammler, head of the Central SS Building Office, to inform the commandant of Auschwitz that the long-awaited giant POW camp at Auschwitz would be constructed next to the parent camp. Its construction was to house many of the new Soviet POWs, and the environment in which they were to be placed would ensure that large numbers of them would perish.

The site chosen for the extension of Auschwitz was near the Polish village of Brzezinka. This marshy tract of land surrounded by birch woods was situated nearly two miles west of the main camp. Although there had never been any concrete plans to construct a massive POW camp on the land, as a precaution, the houses of the small village of Brzezinka were cleared by the SS in July and all its inhabitants relocated elsewhere. The Germans renamed the area Birkenau.

The task of designing Birkenau was left in the capable hands of *SS-Hauptsturmführer* Karl Bischoff, the newly appointed chief of the Auschwitz construction office, and the thirty-three-year-old architect *SS-Rottenführer* Fritz Ertl. The total budget for the

14. To the left of the prefabricated wooden guard tower is the SS hospital building. This building overlooked the camp's crematorium, which can be identified by the tall brick built chimney. In the summer of 1940, this building was to primarily function as a crematorium but it would also serve for prisoner delousing purposes. Before the crematorium came into operation, those who died at the camp were transported to Gliwice and incinerated in the municipal crematorium. The conversion of the crematorium was undertaken with the full authorisation of the SS Construction Management. [Courtesy of the HITM ARCHIVE & Auschwitz-Birkenau Museum]

construction was to be 8.9 million *Reich Marks*. The projected number of prisoners to be housed in the camp was 97,000. It was planned that Birkenau would be divided into a two-part camp, with the smaller part of only 17,000 inmates located in a quarantine camp. The accommodation was to be very overcrowded and initial plans for one barrack block was to contain 550 inmates. This amount was soon altered to a final figure of 744.

In the quarantine camp it was planned that there were going to be two delousing stations, two kitchens, thirty barracks each accommodating 744 men, five toilet barracks, and five washrooms. In the main part of the installation, the camp was to be divided into twelve camps, each with twelve barracks, one kitchen, one toilet barracks, and one washroom. All inmates were to be housed in 174 barracks, each barrack subdivided into sixty-two bays, and each bay having a three-bunkbed system.

In order to build the new camp Russian POWs would be used for slave labour. Almost as soon as the Russian POWs arrived in Auschwitz they were ordered to work. Those that were too weak were killed and disposed of in the crematorium, whilst the remaining prisoners were dragged from their barracks and marched the

15. In its present state showing the northwest side of Crematorium I in the Auschwitz main camp. In September 1944 the crematorium was shut down, its chimney removed and was converted into an air raid shelter for the SS hospital. The chimney was re-built in 1946/47. Note the steel-faced, gas-tight door with peephole. [Courtesy of the HITM ARCHIVE & Auschwitz-Birkenau Museum]

forty minutes to the Birkenau construction site. The first job was to dismantle the existing village and then start building the camp. The Russians had not been given any tools with which to demolish the houses. Instead they were required to pull down the buildings with their bare hands and build the barracks in a similar method. The physical condition of the men was appalling, but they were still forced to work. All day long they laboured in terrible freezing temperatures. First they had to level the ground, then drainage ditches had to be dug, and then finally the various brick barracks and prefabricated wooden horse stables had to be constructed. The speed of the work was of utmost importance, and within fourteen days the quarantine camp had been completed. Over the ensuing weeks, construction of the Birkenau site continued. Many of the Soviet workers laboured for hours in terrible freezing conditions. An outbreak of dysentery had caused numerous problems, and because they were unable to leave their place of work they often soiled their own ragged clothes. Caked in thick mud and faeces the Russian inmates were forced to work, many of them too weak to show any sign of human dignity. At the end of November snow began to fall and the arctic temperatures dramatically increased the number of fatalities. The conditions had become so dreadful that the prisoners were actually dying on site.

By the end of 1941 Auschwitz had slowly transformed from a quite backwater quarantine camp in south western Poland, into one of the largest concentration camp systems of the *Reich*. In little over a year Auschwitz had developed into a dual function camp with many of the inmates that were sent there now living and working. The SS innovative skills too had produced an institution of brutality where it frequently killed others.

Chapter Two
Auschwitz-Birkenau

During late 1941 and early 1942 the SS at Auschwitz had received growing reports on the escalating policies against the Jews in the East, especially by those of the *Einsatzgruppen* (Operational Groups). Since the summer of 1941 Himmler had been making preparations for the mass deportation of Jews to the East. By the end of January 1942, following the Wannsee conference which was a meeting chaired to discuss the 'Final Solution' of the Jewish question, the *Reichsführer* ordered that the concentration camp system was to receive over 150,000 Jews.

The first Jews destined for Auschwitz came from a small transport that arrived on 15 February, and were from the Upper Silesian town of Beuthen. The majority of them was elderly, and because they had already been deemed unfit for work they were immediately led to the camp's crematorium, and killed.

16. A photograph taken inside one of the SS offices at the Auschwitz main camp. [Courtesy of the Auschwitz-Birkenau Museum]

17. Most probably Birkenau, close to the birch woods between the western portion of the camp and the Vistula River. A director of the SS Construction Administration Auschwitz (SS-Zentralbauleitung) Karl Bischoff (left) and Walter Dejaco, his assistant. [Courtesy of the Auschwitz-Birkenau Museum]

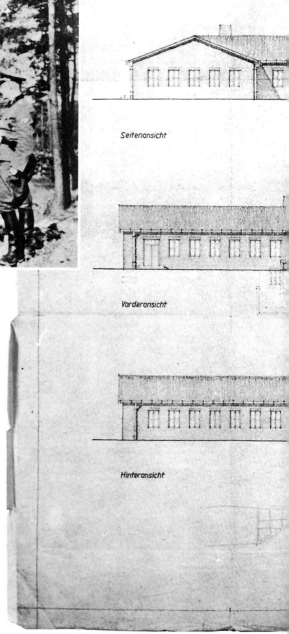

Desinfektions-u. Entwesun

Maßstab 1:100.

Seitenansicht

Vorderansicht

Hinteransicht

18. A blue print showing the construction plans of what became known as the Central Sauna. The building was the most comprehensive disinfection and disinfestation facility built at Birkenau. It was designed following the typhus epidemic that ravaged the camp during July and August 1942. The first drawings were submitted in November 1942, but work on the actual construction project was not completed until late 1943. [Courtesy of the Auschwitz-Birkenau Museum]

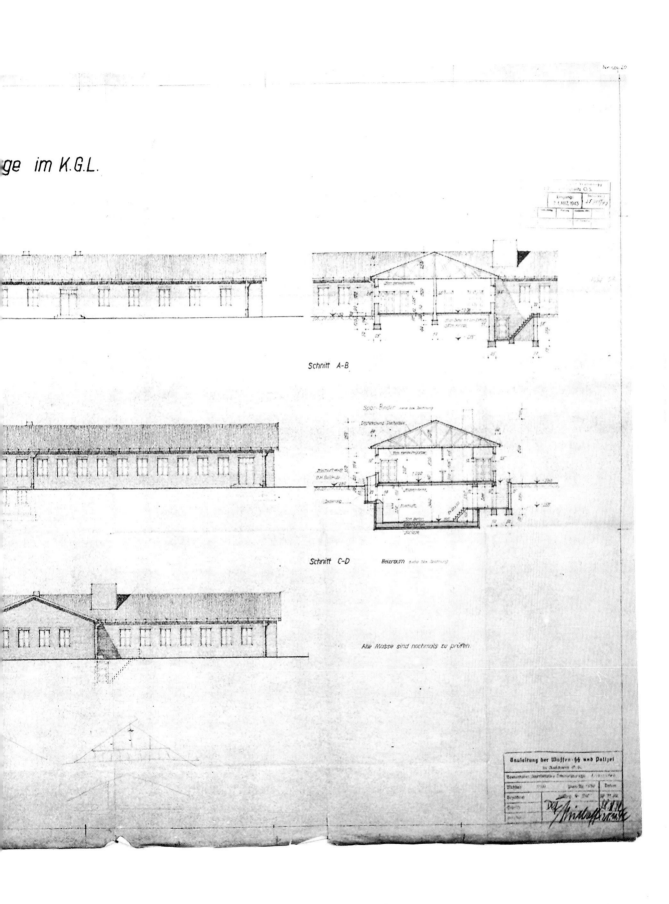

ge im K.G.L.

Schnitt A-B

Schnitt C-D   Heizraum

Alle Masse sind nochmals zu prüfen.

19. A photograph taken at what was known as Auschwitz. I during a visit by Gauleiter Bracht. Rudolf Höss can be seen pictured third from right. [Courtesy of the Auschwitz-Birkenau Museum]

The increased killing in the crematorium was not an ideal situation. In Höss's opinion, it certainly did not favour sending convicted criminals and unfit labour, even if they were Jews, to the already overworked crematorium. If they were to open Birkenau with a large influx of Jews, then Auschwitz would need to improve its cremation facility. It had already been proposed building another crematorium in the base camp alongside the existing one. But if Birkenau was to follow the same crooked path to murder, as Auschwitz had done with the Soviet POWs, it was unquestionably easier installing a crematorium at Birkenau. Höss chaired a meeting with his staff concerning the dilemma. If new policies towards the Jews meant they were now being shipped to the concentration camps, then they would need sufficient tools to dispose of those unfit for work. It was soon decided that the cottage known as Bunker I and nicknamed 'The Little Red House', should be converted as quickly as possible. As part of the conversion, its windows and doors were to be bricked up, edges sealed with felt in order to ensure it was air tight, and the interior gutted to form two rooms. The doors to both rooms were to have a sign attached over the entrance, *'Zur Desinfektion'* (To Disinfection).

Bunker I was completed within a few weeks and on 20 March was made operational for the first time. Jews unfit for work from Upper Silesia had been chosen locally for what the SS authorities were now calling 'special treatment'. Under the cover of darkness the Jews were transported direct to Birkenau.

Despite the panic among some of the elderly Jews, the SS confirmed that the first gassing operation in Birkenau had been a complete success. Most of the Jews had calmly filed into the 'The Little Red House' with no trouble caused to the normal operation of camp life. Although they had solved the problem of how to kill in relative secret, their only concern now was how to dispose of the evidence. Without the advantages of a crematorium on site the only short-term solution was to have the corpses buried in a nearby pit.

The first trainloads of prisoners assigned to Birkenau consisted of 999 able-bodied Slovakian women Jews. The long train steamed its way into Auschwitz on 26 March 1942, and the Jews were unloaded from ramps just outside the station. For many that disembarked from the crammed cattle cars that day the railway stop was very much

20. This photograph is probably taken in the summer of 1943 showing the SS Central Construction Authority in Auschwitz. (*SS-Zentralbauleitung der Waffen SS und Polizei Auschwitz*) [Courtesy of the Auschwitz-Birkenau Museum]

21. Reichsführer Heinrich Himmler visited Auschwitz-Birkenau in March 1941 and then again in July 1942. Here in this photograph he converses with some of the representatives from the giant industrial chemical conglomerate, I.G. Farben, which was proposing the construction of a synthetic-rubber factory near Auschwitz. It would produce a synthetic rubber called Buna and inmates from Auschwitz would erect the building, and be used a slave labour. The project was very lucrative for the SS. [Courtesy of the Auschwitz-Birkenau Museum]

like any other provincial railway station. But this was far removed from anything they had ever endured. Under strict supervision of SS guards, Kapos and local police they were routed through the town of Auschwitz directly to the main camp. All of the Jews had been ordered by the SS to run in groups of five. Those unable to run were simply killed on the spot. Because Birkenau was still under construction Höss had been reluctantly forced to house these women in the main camp, where they were herded into ten specially adapted walled-off barracks. The following day they were ordered to have their heads shaved and were told to wear old Russian uniforms. The uniforms were in abundant supply for nearly 9,000 POWs had so far perished of hunger, illness, malnutrition and various acts of brutality. Housing the Slovakian Jews in the main camp

22. Prisoners from Auschwitz-Birkenau on a work detail being escorted along a road. They are wearing the distinctive blue-and-white-striped uniforms. These are male prisoners as they can be identified wearing hats. Female prisoners were sometimes required to wear headscarves. [Courtesy of the Auschwitz-Birkenau Museum]

23. Workers can be seen digging a trench system in front of the horse stable barracks at Auschwitz-Birkenau. A German company had designed the standard army horse stable barracks and this was produced and dispatched to Auschwitz as a kit that could easily be erected and dismantled. [Courtesy of the Auschwitz-Birkenau Museum]

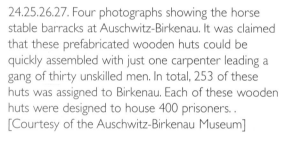

24.25.26.27. Four photographs showing the horse stable barracks at Auschwitz-Birkenau. It was claimed that these prefabricated wooden huts could be quickly assembled with just one carpenter leading a gang of thirty unskilled men. In total, 253 of these huts was assigned to Birkenau. Each of these wooden huts were designed to house 400 prisoners. . [Courtesy of the Auschwitz-Birkenau Museum]

28. One of the brick barracks constructed at Auschwitz-Birkenau. In late 1941, in little over five weeks, some 86,000 cubic feet of brickwork had been erected, using some 1.1 million bricks. Initially, much of the construction was undertaken using brick as there was no wood available. . [Courtesy of the Auschwitz-Birkenau Museum]

29. With the aid of a crane prisoners can be seen digging drainage ditches in Birkenau. The site was situated on marshy land, with the ground only slightly higher than the Vistula and Sola rivers. This meant that rain, melting snow and floodwaters would neither drain into the river nor be absorbed back into the earth. As a consequence hundreds of prisoners were set to work digging vast drainage ditches. [Courtesy of the Auschwitz-Birkenau Museum]

30. Winter of 1943 – 1944 showing the prefabricated wooden stable barracks at B II of the Birkenau camp. [Courtesy of the Auschwitz-Birkenau Museum]

31. Construction works by the main entrance to Birkenau, the photo taken from the internal part of the camp, possibly during the late winter or early spring 1943. Some months later in May 1944 Rudolf Höss would supervise the laying of a railway line through the main entrance for 'Aktion Höss'. [Courtesy of the Auschwitz-Birkenau Museum]

was an administrative nightmare for Höss. There had been no proper preparation for their arrival, which consequently led to numerous problems. Living conditions there had already deteriorated to such a point that there were growing concerns of a typhus epidemic.

In Birkenau conditions were considerably worse than in the main camp. Birkenau had been officially in operation since early March with the remaining Soviet POWs, a group of German criminals, and 1,200 sick prisoners incarcerated in the area designated for the women, officially known as BA I. It was here that the Slovak transport was soon to be moved. In March Birkenau was like a quagmire. There was hardly any water and washing facilities, and the weak and starving prisoners were living in utter filth and degradation. But despite the abysmal circumstances that the prisoners continually endured Höss was eager to send as many inmates to the new camp as possible, for Auschwitz. I was overflowing with prisoners. Here at Birkenau the site would soon be able to house literally thousands of inmates, many of them Jews.

32.33. Two photographs showing prisoners digging drainage ditches at Auschwitz-Birkenau. They were forced to work despite their appallingly bad physical condition. As a consequence many died from hard labour or disease. By July 1942, the Birkenau site had been completely transformed, with several drainage ditches completed. [Courtesy of the Auschwitz-Birkenau Museum]

Throughout the spring and summer of 1942 Bunker I together with Crematorium I in the main camp simultaneously continued to operate killing convicted criminals and those unfit for work. But in spite of this increased killing the SS was still not happy with its efficiency. In order to facilitate the transports arriving at the camp the SS held a meeting with *SS-Sturmbannführer* Karl Bischoff and other members of the Auschwitz Construction Office to discuss plans to convert a second cottage known as the 'Little White House', into what he called a 'bathing facility for special actions'. By the end of June this quiet and unobtrusive looking house, known as Bunker II, went into operation. The interior of the cottage comprised of four narrow rooms that were constructed as gas chambers. With better ventilation and a killing capacity of around 1,200 people at any one time, the SS was sure that Birkenau would run efficiently as never before. As the last finishing touches were made to Bunker II more shipments of Jews were destined for Auschwitz.

On 4 July the first transport of 1,000 Jews arrived outside Birkenau and was submitted for selection. The transports were unloaded at a side-line at Birkenau. In total, 108 able-bodied women and 264 able-bodied men were chosen for work, whilst

34.40. Two photographs clearly showing the cramped conditions inside the barracks. Each barrack was subdivided into sixty-two bays, and each bay had a three-level bunk-bed system. These buildings were primitive and hastily thrown together and caused the death rate to steadily climb. [USHMM - Courtesy of the Yad Vashem Museum]

35. Female prisoners being led away in the snow. These women look relatively elderly and it is probable that they would have been deemed unfit for labour and condemned to the death within a short period of time. [Courtesy of the Auschwitz-Birkenau Museum]

the remaining 638 people were herded off under the cover of darkness to barracks where the victims undressed and then went naked to the gas chambers. All through the procedure the victims were told calmly that they were to bathe and be deloused. Once crammed inside the gas chamber and the doors shut *SS-Unterscharführer* Moll, dressed in a special white protective suit with gas mask, threw the saturated Zyklon B pellets through a little vent, and then waited twenty-five minutes until all the screams of those fighting for their lives fell silent. During the gassing procedure SS surgeons, on duty in the camp, regularly waited nearby with an SS hospital orderly with an oxygen apparatus to revive SS men, in case any of them were to succumb to the poisonous fumes. Once they were certain that all inside were dead the doors and the windows were then opened to ventilate the rooms. The tangled corpses were later removed by the *Sonderkommando* for disposal.

Scenes like this became a common occurrence at Birkenau. SS officers regularly watched the shipments arrive and became morbidly fascinated by the spectacle. They witnessed the selection process at the unloading ramps and saw for themselves first-

37. Rudolf Höss, the commandant of Auschwitz, pictured front right taking SS-Reichsführer Heinrich Himmler on a guided tour of the I.G. Farben site near the village of Monowitz. The construction of the I.G. Farben enterprise was an enormous undertaking, but Himmler was determined to use Auschwitz's increased pool of labour to ensure its rapid completion. [Courtesy of the Auschwitz-Birkenau Museum]

hand the awful scenes of families being torn apart, the separating of the men from the women and children.

Faced with such a grim task of annihilation the SS was now supposed to bury all those killed in Bunker I and Bunker II. Höss was totally aware that this was an inadequate method of body disposal, but he had no other choice. Literally thousands of bodies from both cottages were disposed of in this manner. From the gas chamber entrance the corpses would be loaded onto a truck and driven to the pit and dumped. Powdered lime would be thrown over the bodies and then covered with soil. Already there were some 107,000 corpses that had been buried in Birkenau that were decomposing and polluting the ground water. June and July had been particular hot months and during the first week of July the buried corpses had started to putrefy. The rotting bodies were rising to the surface and there was a terrible stench across the camp. Plagues of rats too were seen gnawing at the corpses and there was evidence of the first cases of typhus fever in the communal camp of the civilian workers deployed in Birkenau. The smell in the camp was terrible. Where the corpses had been buried the whole area was covered with swarms of flies and where the decomposed bodies had been dumped, traces of stinking body fluids oozed out of the holes. In order to remedy the problem Höss installed a giant open cremation area and hoped once and for all his dirty work could be burnt to ashes. A massive large hole was dug and wooden beams acting as a grill were placed across at ground level. Höss had thus improvised a makeshift crematorium whilst waiting for the proper one nearby to be delivered. At once a number of special units consisting of 1,400 prisoners were

38. A group of relatively healthy prisoners that appear to have only just arrived at Auschwitz are seen here at roll-call. These men have been spared immediate death by being selected for labour. However, they were immediately stripped of their individual identities by having their hair shaved off and a registration number tattooed on their left forearm. Men were forced to wear striped clothing, and women wore work dresses. Both were issued ill-fitting work shoes, sometimes clogs. They had no change of clothing and slept in the same clothes they worked in. [Courtesy of the Auschwitz-Birkenau Museum]

39. SS Guards at Auschwitz during a ceremony. At Auschwitz these guards soon learnt the trade of brutality, and all compunction towards mankind was obliterated. Many had already arrived indoctrinated into an almost fanatical determination to serve the SS with blind allegiance. [Courtesy of the Auschwitz-Birkenau Museum]

42. 43. Two photographs showing members of the SS female auxiliaries (*Helferinnen*) and SS officer Karl Hocker who can be seen standing next to the women eating bowls of blueberries. These photographs were taken at an SS retreat called Solahuette not far from Auschwitz. [Courtesy of the USHMM]

44.45. Two photographs showing SS officers, SS female auxiliaries and wives with their children relaxing at the Solahuette retreat. Throughout the evolution of Auschwitz a close-knit community developed amongst the camp's staff and their families; the guards' wives visited one another, gossiped, held afternoon tea parties, and invited their husbands along for evening drinks and dinner. As for the children, they attended private schools in Kattowitz and the surrounding areas, or alternatively the services of a governess were employed. When the children were not attending school they were looked after by domestic slaves, who cooked their meals and cleaned their nicely furnished homes. [Courtesy of the USHMM]

46. A view of the SS retreat at Solahuette. This timber framed building was regarded as an idyllic location for the SS officers' staff of Auschwitz to spend time relaxing and joking. It was a far cry from the horrors less than thirty miles away. [Courtesy of the USHMM]

47. Relaxing among female company and an unidentified officer, the commandant of Auschwitz, Rudolf Höss, can be seen pictured wearing a white suite. [USHMM - Courtesy of the Yad Vashem Museum]

49. 50. Two photographs showing SS troops marching along a road very near to Auschwitz. For many SS guards, their posting to Auschwitz was preferable to having to fight the growing might of the Red Army on the Eastern front.
[Courtesy of the USHMM]

ordered to disinter the bodies with their bare hands. The job was horrific. Because of disease and the unbearable smell many used handkerchiefs and rags to cover their mouth and nose as they dug into the blood filled soil. A huge fire was built with wood and petrol and the corpses were simply thrown on to the enormous pyre of burning rags, flesh and bone.

The already terrible state of affairs was made worse by the typhus epidemic, which by the second week of July had spread to the prisoners of Birkenau. Sanitary conditions were rapidly worsening, mortality rate among able-bodied prisoners were rising, the Jewish transports were arriving so frequently that hygienic and sanitary conditions in the camp would worsen to catastrophic levels. To make matters worse the crematorium in the main camp had not been functioning properly since early June, because its chimney was worn out. At the beginning of July the crematorium went out of service so that the chimney could be removed and relined.

51. A photograph of three members of the SS female auxiliary unit employed at Auschwitz. In total there were some 55,000 guards who served in Nazi concentration camps; of them about 3,700 were women. In 1942, the first female guards arrived at Auschwitz and Majdanek from Ravensbrück. The year after, the Nazis began conscripting women because of a guard shortage. [Courtesy of the USHMM]

52. An SS officer arrives on a visit to Auschwitz. Many SS officers and party officials came to Auschwitz to see for themselves the progress of the expansion programme of the camp, and to meet with the commandant and other members of staff. They even visited occasionally to see first-hand the extermination process. [Courtesy of the Auschwitz-Birkenau Museum]

53. 54. SS officers including Karl Hocker and SS female auxiliary staff take time away from the killings at Auschwitz on a day trip to the mountains in southern Poland. [Courtesy of the USHMM]

41. Jews have arrived by train and have been unloaded and selected for work detail. Two Jewish women can be seen visibly wearing the Star of David stitched to the left breast of their coat. [Courtesy of the Auschwitz-Birkenau Museum]

55. A familiar sign at Auschwitz-Birkenau. Hundreds of Jewish men, women and children have arrived on the ramps and both sexes are being separated. [Courtesy of the Auschwitz-Birkenau Museum]

56. The ramps of Birkenau have been cleared of Hungarian Jews during 'Aktion Höss' and their belongings have been collected together. In the distance the twin chimneys of Crematoria II and III can be seen in the background to the left and right of the two trains. [Courtesy of the Auschwitz-Birkenau Museum]

57. Hundreds of Jews have arrived on the ramp carrying the only possessions they have left with them. The journey to Auschwitz often lasted for days and weeks in appalling sanitary conditions. In this photograph guards have ordered the new arrivals to carry their belongings with them where they would be separated further down the ramp into sexes. In the distance left to right are Crematoria II and III. [Courtesy of the Auschwitz-Birkenau Museum]

58. 59.60.61.62. Five photographs of Jews unloading from cattle trucks during the transportation of Hungarian Jews to Auschwitz in the summer of 1944. Many young children can be seen in these photographs and all of them would have been deemed unfit for labour. Those unfit for labour were directed immediately to the crematoria, while all able-bodied workers were either interned in Auschwitz or transferred to other camps in the Reich. The number of prisoners selected for labour from each transport varied daily; it could be as low as ten per cent of the total transport, or as high as fifty per cent. But the majority of prisoners who passed through the gates of Birkenau were directly sent to their deaths.

63. 64. 65. Three photographs showing Jewish women and children after the selection process on the ramps. After male and females had been divided children up to the age of fourteen stayed with their mother in the women's camp, and those over fourteen years old with their fathers in the men's camp. [Courtesy of the Auschwitz-Birkenau Museum/USHMM - Yad Vasham]

66. A transport carrying Hungarian Jews has arrived in Auschwitz-Birkenau. This photograph has been taken during the selection process and clearly shows SS officers conversing with some of the new arrivals. Many of the Jews are from the Berehov ghetto. The photograph was taken by Ernst Hofmann or Bernhard Walter of the SS. [Courtesy of the Auschwitz-Birkenau Museum]

67. 68.69.70.71. Five photographs showing a new transport of Hungarian Jews that have just arrived at the camp. During May 1944, some 3,300 Jews were arriving in the camp every day, but this figure rose as high as 4,300 on occasion. On 20 May, for instance, a convoy arrived carrying approximately 3,000 people, of whom 2,000 were unfit for work. The following day, on 21 May, two convoys reportedly arrived from Hungary carrying 6,000 people, of whom only 2,000 were fit for work, and the remainder were sent straight to their deaths. It is more than probable that the majority of Jews in these photographs, especially the mothers and children and the old, were among those that were selected to die. [Courtesy of the Auschwitz-Birkenau Museum]

72. 73. 74. Three photographs taken in late May 1944, showing newly arrived Jewish men from Subcarpathian Rus (Carpatho-Ukraine) await selection on the ramp at Auschwitz-Birkenau. The Star of David can clearly be indentified stitched on the left breast of their coats. [Courtesy of the Auschwitz-Birkenau Museum]

75. New arrivals collect their belongings with the assistance of camp helpers that were employed at Auschwitz to aid all new arrivals and to clear their belongings on the ramps once they had been selected. [Courtesy of the Auschwitz-Birkenau Museum]

76. New arrivals of Jews from Subcarpathian Rus are on the ramp at Auschwitz-Birkenau. Among the many arrivals that day two women can be seen smiling and waving to their male loved ones, clearly not knowing where they have been brought. Behind them is Crematorium. II. [Courtesy of the Auschwitz-Birkenau Museum]

77.78. Two photographs showing Hungarian Jews lined-up on the ramp inside Birkenau in the summer of 1944. Both sexes have been separated: men on one side and women on the other. Preparations are being made for the infamous selections to begin in earnest. [Courtesy of the Auschwitz-Birkenau Museum]

79. Hungarian Jews conversing with some of the German guards on the ramp during selection. [Courtesy of the Auschwitz-Birkenau Museum]

80. Hungarian Jews have been separated into a column of males and stand on the ramp awaiting selection. [USHMM - Courtesy of Yad Vashem Museum]

81. 82.83.84.85.86. Six photographs showing the selection process on the ramp at Auschwitz-Birkenau. Entire families often arrived in Auschwitz, but soon after their arrival they were broken apart. Jews were thrown out of the cattle cars often without their belongings and forced to make two separate lines, men and women/children. SS medical personnel then conducted selections among these lines, sending most victims to the gas chambers where they were usually killed and cremated on the same day. [Courtesy of the Auschwitz-Birkenau Museum/ USHMM - Yad Vashem Museum]

87. Male and female prisoners trudge past the endless lines of wooden barracks. Children can also be seen as well in the picture. By the sight of their physical condition it is clear that they have not been in the camp very long. It is almost certain that the children would have already been selected for death. [Courtesy of the Auschwitz-Birkenau Museum]

88. Women prisoners after selection. These females have been spared by the SS for hard labour. They are probably making their way down to what was known as the Sauna to be disinfected and their hair shaved. [Courtesy of the Auschwitz-Birkenau Museum]

89. New male arrivals await selection on the ramp. The first two rows of men appear to look young and healthy, and would almost certainly be selected for hard labour. The men in the third row, however, appear to be old and would probably been selected for death. [Courtesy of the Auschwitz-Birkenau Museum]

90. 91. Two photographs showing newly selected female prisoners prior to being taken to the Sauna. At the Sauna they entered the undressing room where they were medically examined and had their heads shaved. Their clothes were then sent to the autoclaves or hot air chambers. The prisoners were then ordered to the shower in groups of fifty, received a towel to dry themselves and waited for their disinfected and disinfested clothes that they put on in the dressing room. After a final inspection by the SS they emerged from the Sauna and were escorted to their designated barracks. [Courtesy of the Auschwitz-Birkenau Museum]

92.93.94.95.96. Five photographs showing disinfected and shorn female prisoners after leaving the Sauna. After being shorn, disinfected and showered under the surveillance of the SS, they were then given their disinfected and disinfested clothes and escorted to their designated barracks with a blanket for their bunk. Being shaved stripped the new prisoners of the last vestige of their identity. Virtually all the prisoners now looked alike. [Courtesy of the Auschwitz-Birkenau Museum/ USHMM - Yad Vashem Museum]

Chapter Three
The Extermination Centre

The second half of 1942, the SS discussed how best to enlarge camp Birkenau to a capacity of 200,000 inmates. Karl Bischoff had drawn up a plan of the Birkenau site to include two crematoriums, numbered II and III. The crematorium at the main camp was renamed Crematorium I. Another crematorium, known as Crematorium IV was sketched in next to Bunker I, and Crematorium V next to Bunker II. It was estimated that each crematorium had an incineration capacity of 576 corpses a day. To the SS this appeared more than enough to deal with the high volumes that were pouring into the camp. From inception both Crematoria IV and V were to operate as killing centres. They would have their own gas chambers, morgue, and a furnace hall. The other crematoriums would also be transformed to operate as killing machines. Birkenau, it seemed had finally evolved and was now developing into a factory of death.

97. Taken in August 1942 showing *SS-Sturmbannführer* Karl Bischoff and *SS-Untersturmführer* Walter Dejaco, head of the drawing office, conferring with the aid of a blue print during the initial stages of construction at the Crematoria IV and V sites. In the background civilian workers probably from the firm Lenz & Co, which specialised mainly in site levelling work. [Courtesy of the Auschwitz-Birkenau Museum]

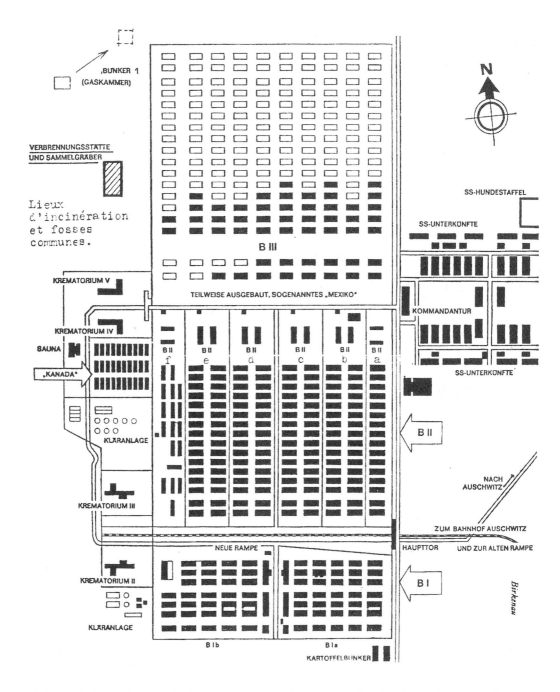

Labels within the map:

,BUNKER 1
(GASKAMMER)

VERBRENNUNGSSTÄTTE
UND SAMMELGRÄBER

Lieux
d'incinération
et fosses
communes.

B III

SS-HUNDESTAFFEL

SS-UNTERKÜNFTE

KREMATORIUM V

KOMMANDANTUR

KREMATORIUM IV

SAUNA

B II f   B II e   B II d   B II c   B II b   B II a

TEILWEISE AUSGEBAUT, SOGENANNTES „MEXIKO"

„KANADA"

SS-UNTERKÜNFTE

KLÄRANLAGE

B II

NACH
AUSCHWITZ

KREMATORIUM III

ZUM BAHNHOF AUSCHWITZ

NEUE RAMPE

HAUPTTOR   UND ZUR ALTEN RAMPE

KREMATORIUM II

B I

KLÄRANLAGE

Birkenau

B Ib   B Ia

KARTOFFELBUNKER

98. A detailed map showing the Birkenau camp in mid-1944. The drawing shows the railway line travelling through to Crematoria II and III. However, due to restrictions on vital materials because of the war this never reached the killing facilities. Those unloaded would have to walk the short distance to their death instead. [Courtesy of the Auschwitz-Birkenau Museum]

99. An Allied aerial reconnaissance photograph taken on 31 May 1944 showing the I.G. Farben Buna camp at Monowitz. This was the largest of the twenty-eight-satellite camps constructed in the Auschwitz zone of interest. By the end of 1943 some 11,000 prisoners were housed in the Monowitz camp, also known as Auschwitz III. [Courtesy of the Auschwitz-Birkenau Museum]

Whilst plans for the new crematoria were drawn-up, Bunkers I and II continued gassing many more Jews. From all over Europe including Slovakia, France, Belgium and the Netherlands Jewish men, women and children were herded through into Birkenau like cattle and sent to their death. Yet in the midst of this horror Auschwitz during this period was still playing only a minor part in the slaughter of the Jews. The major killing centres were already established in the forests of Poland – Belzec, Sobibor and Treblinka. But the final transformation of Auschwitz came on 26 September. Höss received instructions from *SS-Obergruppenführer* Oswald Pohl that all possessions belonging to the majority of prisoners entering Auschwitz were to be confiscated for good, labelled and stored. Initially, all possessions had been stored in Block 26 in the main camp, but there was so much looted property that the Auschwitz authorities

100. Inmates of Birkenau during the construction phase of Crematorium III in late 1942 early 1943. Crematorium III was officially transferred to the camp authorities on 24 June 1943. [Courtesy of the Auschwitz-Birkenau Museum]

were compelled to erect six barracks near to the main camp. From these special storage facilities all foreign currency, valuables, gold and other precious metals were authorised to be transported to SS headquarters in Berlin. Usable clothing, shoes, bed linen, blankets, fabrics, household utensils were to be directed to the Ethnic German Liaison Office and distributed for the use of German settlers. As for unusable clothing and other pieces of material these were instructed to be sent directly to the Reich

101. The construction of Crematorium IV taken by SS-man Kamann in late 1942. The architects signed off Crematorium IV on 22 March 1943, without having time to test the incinerators. After two weeks of intensive use the double four muffle furnace cracked. The incinerator was decommissioned in May 1943. [Courtesy of the Auschwitz-Birkenau Museum]

102. Prisoners working on the construction site for storage of cabbages in 1944. [Courtesy of the Auschwitz-Birkenau Museum]

Ministry of Economy and used for the war effort. It was confirmed that the transportation of all these goods were being planned, and with the amount of Jews destined for Auschwitz the yield would be enormous. Many SS officers saw the scheme as a very lucrative enterprise, not just for the Auschwitz authorities and the government in Berlin, but also for those running the camp.

But whatever thoughts the SS may have had regarding 'all the Jewish treasures', the German authorities were eager to get the construction of the crematoriums installed as quickly as possible. In fact, construction of the crematoriums had already begun in earnest with several hundred workers allocated to building the crematoriums. Despite the massive pool of labour, the Auschwitz construction office knew they would be unable to carry out the building project on its own. Whilst the inmates were capable of building wooden barracks, residential buildings and digging drainage systems, they required civil engineer firms for the actual construction. In total eleven construction companies were involved in the building of all the crematoriums. The civilian firm called Huta from Kattowitz, was already working on the shell of Crematorium II, and then began work on Wednesday 23 September on Crematorium IV. A total of about eighty men worked on the site, sixty or so were prisoners, of which twenty of them worked

103. A photograph of Crematorium IV. From the time of its inception Crematorium IV was to operate as a killing centre. It had its own gas chamber, a morgue and a furnace hall. Work on Crematorium IV began on 23 September 1942. Nine civilian firms in Upper Silesia participated in the construction of Crematorium IV, which were designated during the construction stage as Bauwerke / Worksites 30b and 30c. The main outer shell of the building was constructed by a firm called Huta of Kattowitz and Reidel & Son of Bielitz; the roof was designed by Konrad Segnitz; the chimneys were built by Robert Koehler of Myslowitz; the external sewers and drains were installed by Karl Falck of Gleiwitz and Triton of Kattowitz. Inside the building the eight-muffle furnaces were built by Josef Kluge of Gleiwitz under the direction of the manufacturers, Topf & Sons of Erfurt. Once completed the building was officially handed over by the Bauleitung to the Camp Administration on 22 March 1943, though some further work was carried out from 24 April to 8 May 1943. [Courtesy of the Auschwitz-Birkenau Museum]

for the Auschwitz contractor Koehler on building the chimneys. In total between 100 and 150 persons, of whom the majority were prisoners, were employed on the individual work sites. In order to ensure all the firms worked well together a *Sonderführer* would manage the works in progress and see that the job was completed efficiently and as quickly as possible. For the ensuing weeks and months to come he oversaw firms like Karl Falck from Gleiwitz and the Triton Company from Katowitz that handled the drainage work of Crematoria III, IV, and V. The Klug Company from

Gleiwitz which helped Topf and Sons build the furnaces of Crematoria IV and V. Huta who were contracted to complete the floor and walls of the two underground morgues of Crematorium II, whilst the Vedag Company from Breslau, were paid to waterproof the cellars of Crematorium II and III.

At the end of February 1943 the first of Birkenau's crematoria, Crematorium II, was finally completed and the five triple-muffle furnaces were to be tested. A few days later on 4 March forty-five 'well-fleshed' male corpses specially selected from a batch gassed in Bunker II were transported to Crematorium II. The incineration rooms were on the ground floor, while in the cellar there was a gas chamber and a mortuary. Inside the incineration room the bodies were cremated under the watchful eye of Prüfer and other engineers. For the next ten days the furnaces were run to dry them out whilst engineers completed the gas chamber ventilation system. On Saturday 13 March, it was announced that Crematorium II was officially operational and ready for 'special treatment'. During the evening of Sunday 14 March, 1,492 women, children, and old people from the Krakow ghetto had been selected for the trial run at Crematorium II. Under the cover of darkness the Jews were quietly led to a temporary undressing hut built next to Crematorium II in its north yard.

104. Crematorium V in 1943. Work on Crematorium V started on 15 November 1942, and it was officially handed over on 4 April 1943, but it was not actually operational until 18 April and work was not completed on worksite 30c until 22 April. However, during the first weeks of working the furnaces were not operated correctly, being constantly overheated. Topf & Sons blamed the Sonderkommando for deliberately damaging the internal lining with their fire irons. [Courtesy of the Auschwitz-Birkenau Museum]

105. A photograph of the sedimentation basin of BA I, in the summer of 1943. North of the sedimentation basin is Crematorium II with its blackened chimney clearly seen. By mid 1943, it was estimated that Crematoria II and III burned an average of 1,440 bodies per day. [Courtesy of the Auschwitz-Birkenau Museum]

106. Crematorium III probably in the spring of 1944. Reports reveal that between April and September in 1943, Crematorium III worked for only two months at full capacity. Only a quarter of their maximum capacity was utilised. Nonetheless, in the midst of all these technical problems an enormous amount of people were still sent to their deaths. From 25 June 1943 to 27 November 1944, Crematorium III killed about 350,000 victims. [Courtesy of the Auschwitz-Birkenau Museum]

SS officers watched as the Jews under the supervision of the *Sonderkommando* were ordered to undress, and kindly requested to keep their personal effects together for when they returned. They were then led naked in file down the western stairway, with its metal guard rails to the basement of Crematorium II through a doorway with a sign that read *'Bath and Disinfection Room'*. As they entered the room they could see that from the ceiling hung sieves mounted on pieces of wood or metal, which appeared to be shower heads. Once crammed inside, the airtight door to the room was slammed shut and secured by two latch bars, which were screwed tight. So that the killing process could be observed, there was a specially designed peephole consisting of a double pane of glass. Through this opening the SS watched as 1 or 1.5kg of pale blue-green granulated Zyklon B was poured in from the roof by SS medical orderlies

107. Prisoners pour concrete for the ceiling of the underground undressing hall of Crematorium II at Auschwitz-Birkenau in the winter of 1943. [Courtesy of the Auschwitz-Birkenau Museum]

108. The construction of Crematorium IV taken by SS-man Kamann in late 1942. The architects signed off Crematorium IV on 22 March 1943, without having time to test the incinerators. After two weeks of intensive use the double four-muffle furnace cracked. The incinerator was decommissioned in May 1943. [Courtesy of the Auschwitz-Birkenau Museum]

109. A photograph of Crematorium IV taken probably in September or October 1942. The main outer shell of the building is clearly being constructed along with one of the Crematorium's chimneys. The main outer shell of the building was constructed by the firm Huta of Kattowitz and Reidel & Son of Bielitz, whilst the chimneys were built by Robert Koehler of Myslowitz. [Courtesy of the Auschwitz-Birkenau Museum]

110. On the ramp after selection. These Hungarian Jews have been selected for death and wait to be escorted to the Crematoria. In the distance is Crematorium II. On Saturday, 13 March, it was announced that Crematorium II was officially operational and ready to begin administering what the SS referred to as 'special treatment'. On the evening of Sunday, 14 March, a total of 1,492 women, children, and elderly people from the Krakow ghetto had been selected for the trial run in Crematorium II. That night Jewish prisoners were quietly led to a temporary undressing hut that had been erected next to Crematorium II in the north yard, and then gassed. [Courtesy of the Auschwitz-Birkenau Museum]

112. A long column of women and children including the old are led away down towards Crematorium II to a fate that can only be imagined. In little under an hour, pending on the volume of people that entered the camp that day, all those regarded as 'unfit for work', were led down to the Crematorium and filed into what was known as the central room and undressed there in preparation for gassing. [USHMM - Courtesy of Yad-Vashem Museum]

113. Hungarian male Jews wait to be led into the Crematorium and gassed. They are under the impression that they are waiting to be showered and disinfected before rejoining their family and friends. [USHMM - Courtesy of Yad-Vashem Museum]

114.115.116.117. Four photographs showing Hungarian women with their children being led through the camp to the Crematorium to be gassed. Frequently there were so many people that had been selected for death that often long queues were formed, where Jews had to patiently sit or stand around waiting to go through. [USHMM - Courtesy of Yad-Vashem Museum]

wearing gas masks. It entered the room via four metal-meshed hollow columns that protruded from the concrete ceiling. When the gas was dropped into the room the victims started screaming and panicking, but their death agonies were not heard for long because the Zyklon B used was forty times the lethal dose. In a few minutes, five at the most, the gas chamber fell silent. Once they were sure that all the victims were no longer moving the air extraction system was then switched on for at least twenty or thirty minutes so that it could suck out the poisoned air that was still in the chamber. The gas-tight door was then unbolted and opened, and then the gruesome task of extracting the dead women, children and old people began immediately by the *Sonderkommando*. It was noted that many of the dead had their eyes still open and

118. On the selection ramp, it is most probable that these old gentlemen would have been deemed 'unfit' for labour and sent to their death. [USHMM - Courtesy of Yad-Vashem Museum]

119. Mothers with their children on the selection ramp. Throughout this process the SS tried to maintain an element of calmness in order to reduce panic among the Jews. It was for this reason they decided to reluctantly send perfectly fit mothers to the gas chambers in order to soothe their offspring as they were led into the changing rooms. [USHMM - Courtesy of Yad-Vashem Museum]

were hanging onto one another. Some bodies were crushed by the door, whilst others were found lying around the wire mesh columns. It was quite apparent that many people had tried to escape from the columns, making their way in panic to the doorway. Their bodies were covered with scratches and bruises as the victims trampled one another in frantic effort to escape the gas. Many had blood oozing from their noses and mouths with their faces bloated and blue, and some were so deformed they were unrecognizable. Inside the chamber it was very hot and some, in particular the children probably died of suffocation before the gassing, due to the lack of air. The corpses were then loaded three or four times on a temporary hoist, and

120. On the selection ramp, Hungarian Jews are being selected by Nazi doctors. A truck can be seen parked on the ramp in preparation to carry disabled or old people direct to the Crematoriaum without delaying the extermination process. It was also used to transport people's belongs direct to the Canada buildings. Note in the distance a large column of Jews being led down towards Crematoria II and III. [Courtesy of the Auschwitz-Birkenau Museum]

121. On the selection ramp, and this photograph was taken moments before (image 120), showing the selection process. SS officers, guards and Nazi doctors can be seen selecting Jews and ensuring that they join the correct queue. [Courtesy of the Auschwitz-Birkenau Museum]

sent up to the ground floor. Plans for the installation of an electric elevator had already been drawn-up. Once the bodies arrived on the ground floor of the incinerator room the *Sonderkommando* attached leather thongs to the bodies and pulled them along the concrete surface through shallow water to a point in front of the furnaces. They were then placed face up head to foot in threes on a metal 'corpse board' that ran on rollers and rammed into one of the muffles. It was predicted that the incineration process would probably take between forty-five minutes and one hour, but that evening the incinerators were only being run at half its capacity to prevent any technical problems. In total, preparation and gassing took two hours, but the incineration took nearly forty-eight hours.

A few weeks later Crematorium IV was also run simultaneously with Crematorium II. On 4 April, Crematorium V was officially handed over to the camp administration, but the installation was still not deemed fully operational, since the gas-tight doors to the gas chambers were still to be fitted. Work on the doors was completed between 16 and 17 April by a civilian firm working for Huta. There was now a great urgency to complete the other two crematoria. On 24 June, Crematorium III was transferred to the camp authorities. By the end of June Auschwitz-Birkenau had an official daily incineration output of some 4,756 corpses. Yet, despite frequent requests by the engineers not to overload the crematorium, the Auschwitz authorities continued to operate the installations at their absolute limit. By early July the transports to Auschwitz-Birkenau had become much larger and the number of people selected for 'special treatment' increased massively.

During July and August recurring problems with the crematoria still continued to hamper operations. With all four crematoria running simultaneously Auschwitz had a

122. A tragic image of an elderly lady trudging along a road with children destined for the crematoria in the summer of 1944. [USHMM - Courtesy of Yad-Vashem Museum]

123. 124. 125. 126. 127. 128. 129. 130. Eight photographs showing Hungarian Jews in the summer of 1944, that have been selected to die waiting in the grove of trees by Crematoria IV and V. Scenes like this were a common occurrence at Auschwitz-Birkenau, especially during the liquidation of the Hungarian transports between May and July 1944. During this period roughly 3,300 Jews were arriving in the camp every day, but this figure rose as high as 4,300 on occasion. Although this action was the most sustained mass killing so far in the history of the Auschwitz camp, and was comparable to the scale of murders carried out at Treblinka during July and August of 1942, it was also the most problematic. There were so many Jews that had been selected to die that frequently hundreds of women and children, including the old, had to sit and wait for some considerable time outside the compound of the crematoria before being ordered to undress and be led through the crematoria to their death. [Courtesy of the Auschwitz-Birkenau Museum/ USHMM - Yad-Vashem Museum]

131. A frightened old Jewish women being constrained by three Jewish men is being led in the grove of trees by Crematoria IV and V. [Courtesy of the Auschwitz-Birkenau Museum]

132. A line of male Jews is being assessed by a Nazi doctor. In just a few moments he will decide who lives and who is to die. Everyone to his right is being led away towards Crematorium II. All those chosen to work are rounded up to his left and led down to the Central Sauna for disinfecting and shorning. [USHMM - Courtesy of the Yad-Vashem Museum]

massive killing potential, and yet only two were in operation. Crematorium IV was out of service and Crematorium II had temporarily stopped working to be repaired. Crematorium I was closed down altogether at the request of the Political Department, and as for Crematoria III and V, these two installations were running, but at full capacity. Höss attempted everything possible to try and speed up the process of killing, fearing the camp would become quickly overcrowded with those destined for 'special treatment'. In fact, reports had confirmed that between April and end of September 1943, Crematoria II, III, IV, and V only worked for two months at full capacity. Only a quarter of their maximum capacity was used. Nonetheless, in the midst of all these problems an enormous amount of people were still sent to their deaths in all four crematoria during this time. In total between 160,000 and 210,000 victims were given 'special treatment'.

133. There were so many Hungarian Jews destined for the crematoria that even the ramps were occasionally filled with Jews waiting to go through to be gassed. Here in this photograph a group of old Jewish men wait on the ramps next to a stationary cattle truck. [Courtesy of the Auschwitz-Birkenau Museum]

134. A young girl stares at the camera unbeknown to her or her family what fate awaits her. The crematoria dressing rooms were often so full that many Jews had to undress naked in the birch of trees and be led in single file straight into the gas chambers. [Courtesy of the Auschwitz-Birkenau Museum]

135.136.137.138.139.140.141. Seven photographs showing inmates loading up trucks of the possessions left by Jews on the ramps after the selection process. All these possessions were transported to the camp storage facility known as 'Canada'. During the first half of 1942 a special storage facility was opened, which the inmates nicknamed 'Canada', and in time this name was adopted by the guards. Canada consisted of six barracks and was situated about 500 metres from the main camp. Some 1,500 prisoners were responsible for sorting through the looted property in shifts. In December 1943, a much bigger warehouse, known as Canada II, was opened on a site between Crematoria II and III and Crematoria IV and V at Birkenau. Canada II comprised thirty permanently overflowing wooden barracks. [Courtesy of the Auschwitz-Birkenau Museum/ USHMM - Yad-Vashem Museum]

142. 143. Two photographs showing the deadly crystallised prussic acid, which was sold in tins labeled 'Zyklon B'. Depending on the weather conditions, between five and seven kilograms of pale, blue-green granulated Zyklon B would have been poured into the crematoria's gas chamber by SS medical orderlies wearing gas masks. This quantity of Zyklon B could kill between 1,500 and 2,000 people. The gas entered the room via four metal-meshed hollow columns protruding from the concrete ceiling and would have killed everyone within minutes. [Courtesy of the Auschwitz-Birkenau Museum]

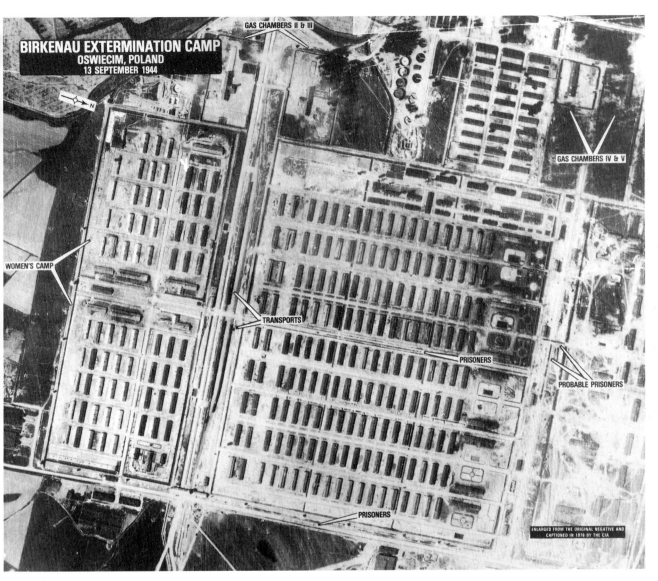

144. An Allied aerial reconnaissance photograph taken on 13 September 1944 showing Auschwitz-Birkenau, also known as Auschwitz II. The photograph clearly identifies all the camp's crematoria, transport and probable prisoners or camp personnel. [Courtesy of the Auschwitz-Birkenau Museum]

Labels within image:

SOLA RIVER

AUSCHWITZ I
OSWIECIM, POLAND
14 JANUARY 1945

"BLOCK 10"
"MEDICAL EXPERIMENTS"

"BLOCK 11"
PENAL BARRACKS

TO BIRKENAU

145. An Allied aerial reconnaissance photograph taken on 14 January 1945 showing the main camp Auschwitz I. The Höss family residence house sits at the end of the block barracks nearest to the road overlooking the Sola River. [Courtesy of the Auschwitz-Birkenau Museum]

Chapter Four
The End

By 1944, with death camps like Kulmhof, Sobibor, Belzec, and Treblinka now closed down, it was up to the other camps, in particular Auschwitz-Birkenau, to take responsibility for the remnants of the Jewish communities of Poland, France, the Netherlands, Italy and the rest of occupied Europe. Hungary was one particular country that still had the largest amount of Jews. Almost 725,000 Jews were still on Hungarian territory, and for the German government that figure was too much an opportunity to resist. When the German occupation forces rolled across into Hungary on 19 March, Himmler now wanted the Hungarian Jews transported to Auschwitz where they would be selected for slave labour and shipped out again through the various concentration camps that served the German industry. Those that were selected for labour would be held in quarantine until transport was made readily available to them. In effect, the *Reichsführer* was planning to turn Auschwitz into a huge labour exchange, just as he had done with the main camp in 1940. But now it was on a greater scale than ever before. The Auschwitz authorities were informed that they

146. Three SS officers study a document during the dedication of the new SS hospital. Pictured left to right are Dr Enno Lolling, Commandant Richard Baer and Adjutant Karl Hocker. [Courtesy of USHMM ARCHIVES]

147. SS officers including Rudolf Höss watch as Commandant Baer exchanges documents with Karl Bischoff during the dedication of the new SS hospital in Auschwitz. [Courtesy of USHMM ARCHIVES]

were to prepare for a huge assignment of Hungarian Jews. They were also told that more of an effort was to be made to separate those Jews who could serve the German war effort through work, but were to continue to use 'special treatment' on those that served absolutely no purpose for the *Reich*.

The first transport of Hungarian Jews, consisting of 1,800 people, had arrived in Birkenau in early May, but Höss was expecting many more convoys over the ensuing weeks to come. In preparation for their arrival he immediately set to work and ordered that Crematorium V be put into operation again. An engineer's report, however, confirmed that Crematorium V furnaces were still damaged, and because of their slow incineration rate they had replaced them in late April by five small incineration ditches. In order to compensate the huge numbers of transports expected over the coming weeks it was suggested to reactivate Bunker II, and designate it as Bunker 2/V. Höss agreed, because from his past experiences at the camp it was not actually the process of killing the Jews that presented him and his SS colleagues with any problems; the hardest task was disposing of the gassed victims. So that he could facilitate the process of murder quickly and effectively he made *SS-Hauptsturmführer* Otto Moll in charge of all four crematoria, and assigned a special squad to enlarge the inside of the crematoria. From Crematorium V a special track was laid between the building and the pits so that the corpses could be loaded onto trolleys and disposed of quickly. As for the other killing installations, they were also overhauled including Crematoria II and III, which received new elevators connecting

148. SS officers gather for the dedication ceremonies of the new SS hospital. Pictured in the centre is Commandant Richard Baer. From November 1942 until May 1944, Baer was adjutant of SS-Obergruppenführer Oswald Pohl, then chief of the *Wirtschaftsverwaltungshauptamt* (SS office of economic policy). In November 1943, he took over command of department D I, the Inspectorate for Concentration Camps. He succeeded Arthur Liebehenschel, considered by Himmler to be too soft with the prisoners, as the third and final commandant of Auschwitz from 11 May 1944, until early 1945. [Courtesy of USHMM ARCHIVES]

149. Guards stand at attention during the dedication of the new SS hospital in Auschwitz. [Courtesy of USHMM ARCHIVES]

150. SS officers and SS physicians arrive for the dedication of the new SS hospital at Auschwitz. [Courtesy of USHMM ARCHIVES]

the gas chambers with the incineration rooms. Even the walls of the changing rooms and the gas chambers were given a fresh coat of paint.

To assist the smooth arrival of the Hungarian Jews and to provide a direct link between the Auschwitz station and the crematoria the train lines were extended through the main entrance of Birkenau with plans to run them right up to Crematoria II and III. Night and day hundreds of prisoners had been busy laying the three-way railway track through the camp, and constructing the loading and unloading ramps. By the second week of May the railway line was completed and the finishing touches were made to the ramps. From these ramps Höss would now coordinate the destruction of the Hungarian Jews, now code-named 'Aktion Höss'.

The first major Hungarian transports steamed their way through to Auschwitz on 15 May. Once they arrived the train pulled over the new spur through the gate into Birkenau and halted at the ramps. Here at the ramps 'Aktion Höss' was put into

151. A soldier salutes an officer, while several other officers stand in the background during the dedication of a new SS hospital in Auschwitz. Pictured on the left are Dr Eduard Wirths, Commandant Richard Baer and Karl Bischoff. [Courtesy of USHMM ARCHIVES]

operation, firstly unloading of the Jews from the cattle trains. Once the Jews were unloaded they were immediately separated into two columns, one of women and children, the other of men. A selection was then carried out by one or two SS medical doctors and the two columns were divided into four columns; two of women and children, and two of men. Those unfit for labour were sent straight ahead toward the crematoria, whilst all able-bodied workers were interned in Auschwitz, or were retained ready at a moment's notice to be transferred to other camps in the *Reich*. The selection for labour in each transport varied daily, sometimes it was as low as ten per cent, or as high as fifty per cent. But the majority of Jews that arrived through the gates of Birkenau were immediately sent through to the '*bathhouses*' to their death. Roughly there were 3,300 people per day arriving, sometimes that figure even rose to 4,300. On 20 May, for instance, one convoy arrived with an average of 3,000 people of whom some 1,000 were able, and 2,000 were unable to work. The following day on 21 May two convoys were reported to have arrived from Hungary with 6,000

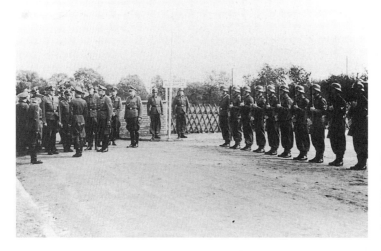

152. SS guards and officers, including Hocker and Höss, during the dedication of the new SS hospital in Auschwitz. [Courtesy of USHMM ARCHIVES]

153. Dr Lolling shakes hands with Dr Eduard Wirths during the dedication of the new SS hospital in Auschwitz. The ceremony marks the transfer of documents and authority from the construction department to the camp upon completion of the project. [Courtesy of USHMM ARCHIVES]

people of whom 2,000 were able to work and the remainder were directly sent to their death. During that day both the incinerators of Crematoria II and III were being serviced so the victims from the transport were disposed of in the three incineration ditches next to Crematorium V. Though the specially built track from the crematorium to the pits had been laid it was never used because it was considered an inconvenience. Instead, the *Sonderkommando* had to drag the corpses directly from the gas chamber to the pits.

As more convoys arrived daily at Birkenau from Hungary Höss was kept continuously informed on its progress. Regularly he visited Birkenau where he watched the selections, and was even seen observing the burning of the corpses in the open-air ditches, ensuring that they were being disposed of quickly, ready for the next arrival. The transports varied daily, but from the very beginning of the '*Aktion*' until midnight

154. Officers watch Commandant Richard Baer shake hands [probably with Karl Bischoff] during the dedication of the new SS hospital in Auschwitz. [Courtesy of USHMM ARCHIVES]

155. SS officers and German nurses gather during the dedication ceremony of the new SS hospital. Among those pictured are Karl Hocker, Josef Kramer and Heinrich Schwarz. In late 1943 early 1944, Schwarz became camp commandant of Auschwitz III Monowitz. While camp commandants at other camps in the complex were removed after only a few months, Schwarz continued to enjoy his superior Oswald Pohl's goodwill. [Courtesy of USHMM ARCHIVES]

on 28 May, it had been reported that some 184,049 Jews had arrived in Auschwitz in fifty-eight trains. Within a period of just two weeks approximately 122,700 persons that were deemed unsuitable for forced labour were subsequently sent to their death. Birkenau was effectively gassing over 8,000 Jews on average each day. For the Auschwitz authorities the numbers were no less impressive for it was the most sustained mass killing so far in the history of the camp, and only comparable to the scale of murders undertaken at Treblinka during July and August 1942.

In order to ensure that the camp would not generate into chaotic disorder the SS increased the numbers of *Sonderkommando* that were working in shifts in the four crematoria. By the end of May there were nearly 900 of these people living and working in the crematoria. The whole of this horrific operation was supervised only by a handful of SS men.

Throughout June more trains continued to arrive from Hungary. Though the operation was a success, the high numbers gassed began to exceed the official incineration capacity, and as a result the crematoria begun overflowing with the dead.

156. SS officers gather for the dedication ceremonies of the new SS hospital. Pictured on the left is Karl Hocker. [Courtesy of USHMM ARCHIVES]

Many victims were already being burned in the pits nearby to cope with the high amount of corpses, but Moll, who oversaw the liquidation of the Hungarian Jews, assured his superiors that the 'Moll Plan' would be achieved swiftly and successfully.

Over the coming weeks an orgy of destruction escalated. Thousands of Hungarian Jews continued their one-way passage to the crematoria, including valuable labour. Höss had observed how families had often fought to stay together during the selections, and watched with fascination how children clung to their mothers, screaming and crying. Instead of wrenching children from their mother's arms he had learnt that the best way to prevent any emotional disturbances was to reluctantly send young and healthy women suitable for hard labour to the gas chambers with their offspring. Many Hungarian women and children went to their deaths in this way.

157. Officers walk towards the dedication of the new SS hospital in Auschwitz. In the centre to the right of Karl Hocker is the former commandant of Auschwitz, Rudolf Höss. [Courtesy of USHMM ARCHIVES]

158. SS officers and German nurses attend the dedication ceremony of the new SS hospital. Among those pictured is Karl Hocker (back, left). [Courtesy of USHMM ARCHIVES]

159. A photograph taken at Auschwitz after the handing over of the new SS hospital. Pictured left to right are Dr Eduard Wirths, Dr Enno Lölling, and Auschwitz commandant Richard Baer. Standing to their left is adjutant Karl Hoecker, and Rudolf Höss. [Courtesy of USHMM ARCHIVES]

160. Another photograph taken at Auschwitz after the handing over of the new SS hospital. Pictured left to right Dr Eduard Wirths, Dr Enno Lölling, Commandant Richard Baer, Adjutant Karl Hoecker and Rudolf Höss. [Courtesy of USHMM ARCHIVES]

No matter how gruesome the outcome was for these hapless Hungarian Jews during the summer of 1944, the SS had created the perfect killing factory on an industrial scale. All four crematoria were now working more or less on a daily basis, killing thousands each day. The ovens continued to work at full capacity and the incineration ditches were being used day and night. The frenetic gassings and burnings carried on for days and weeks regardless of the deteriorating military situation. During July an average of 3,500 each day were arriving at the ramps with more than three-quarters of the new arrivals being sent directly to the crematoria for 'special treatment'. This phenomenal figure certainly demonstrated the SS efficiency to oversee 'Aktion Höss' with a fanatical determination. In no less than eight weeks they had masterminded the killing of more than 320,000 Hungarian Jews. During July Budapest confirmed that the deportations were to be suspended.

Auschwitz had finally evolved, and it was now left in the capable hands of the new commander to start making plans to liquidate whole sections of Birkenau. One particular section that had been discussed was the gypsy camp. At its peak there were estimated to be some 23,000 gypsy men and women in the camp. However, thanks to overcrowding combined with the lack of food and water, disease had quickly spread throughout the camp killing 20,000 of the 23,000 gypsies. Those remaining were rounded up on the night of 2 August and marched off to the crematoria and gassed.

Over the next few months the killings at Auschwitz continued, but as the fighting on the Eastern Front deteriorated and the Russians pushed ever deeper into Poland, the Auschwitz authorities were ordered to cease extermination operations across the *Reich*. At Birkenau the *Sonderkommando* had dismantled all the killing apparatus. The incineration ditches too had been cleared and levelled, and pits which had been filled with ash and crushed bones of murdered prisoners were emptied and covered with

161. After the formal handing over the new SS hospital at Auschwitz Rudolf Höss, seen on the left, strolls with Commandant Baer. [Courtesy of USHMM ARCHIVES]

162. A well-decorated Rudolf Höss is pictured with Commandant Baer and Karl Hocker. [Courtesy of USHMM ARCHIVES]

fresh turf and other plantation. Crematorium I in the main camp had been turned into an air raid shelter and the chimney and holes in the ceiling in which the Zyklon B was thrown in was removed. All the furnaces of Crematoria I, II, III and IV were dismantled and usable parts transported to other camps. On the night of 17 January some 58,000 prisoners were evacuated from Monowitz and the Auschwitz sub-camps, with about 20,000 coming from the Auschwitz-Birkenau camp alone. Very few were evacuated by train, with the majority of them being forced into the snow and marched in freezing night-time temperatures westward towards Germany. As they shuffled along the icy road behind them the night sky lit with flashes and the distant sounds of Russian gunfire rumbled across the horizon. Anyone including children that were unable to

162. Studio portraits of SS officers Richard Baer and Karl Hoecker. The original caption reads "With the Commandant SS Stubaf. Baer, Auschwitz 21.6.44". [Courtesy of USHMM ARCHIVES]

163. Studio portrait of Karl Hocker taken in June 1944. [Courtesy of USHMM ARCHIVES]

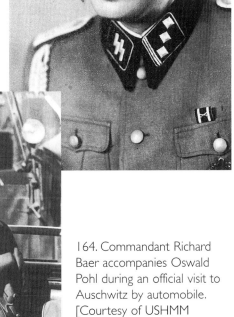

164. Commandant Richard Baer accompanies Oswald Pohl during an official visit to Auschwitz by automobile. [Courtesy of USHMM ARCHIVES]

165. SS officers relax and converse in groups on the grounds of the SS retreat at Solahutte, outside Auschwitz. From left to right: Josef Kramer, (unidentified), Karl Hocker, and Franz Hossler. Just weeks before this photograph was taken, in May 1944, Josef Kramer was put in charge of the gas chambers at the Auschwitz-Birkenau compound. He was to hold that position until December 1944, when he was transferred out as Commandant of Belsen. [Courtesy of USHMM ARCHIVES]

167. Several SS officers study a document during the dedication of the new SS hospital. Pictured left to right are Dr Enno Lolling, Commandant Richard Baer, adjutant Karl Hocker, and former commandant Rudolf Höss. [Courtesy of USHMM ARCHIVES]

168. Two SS officers walk together past a building. Pictured on the left is Karl Hocker. The officer on the right is unidentified. [Courtesy of USHMM ARCHIVES]

169. SS officer Karl Hocker salutes in front of an array of wreaths during a military funeral at Auschwitz. The original caption of the photograph reads 'Burying our SS comrades from a terror attack'. [Courtesy of USHMM ARCHIVES]

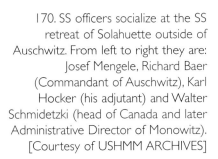

170. SS officers socialize at the SS retreat of Solahuette outside of Auschwitz. From left to right they are: Josef Mengele, Richard Baer (Commandant of Auschwitz), Karl Hocker (his adjutant) and Walter Schmidetzki (head of Canada and later Administrative Director of Monowitz). [Courtesy of USHMM ARCHIVES]

keep pace with the mass exodus was shot and their murdered corpses left at the roadside. The scenes were utterly terrible.

Amidst the chaotic evacuation order, the small groups of SS left behind at Auschwitz were given instructions for the demolition of the crematoria including Bunkers I and II. After having blown up the remaining shells of Crematoria II and III in the early afternoon of 20 January, six days later they dynamited Crematorium V. As for Crematorium IV, this building had been demolished after it had been damaged by fire following a revolt in October 1944 by *Sonderkommando*. During the demolition of the crematoria special SS units murdered around 700 prisoners at Birkenau and nearby sub-camps. As news of the Red Army advanced along the main road from Krakow, the guards were ordered to destroy the last of the camp records, set fire to the Canada stores and liquidate the remaining prisoners in the camp. However, more concerned with saving their own lives than following orders the SS guards fled the camp leaving the soldiers of the First Ukrainian Front to liberate Auschwitz and its sub-camps.

171. SS officers, some with cigars in hand, socialize on the grounds of the SS retreat Solahuette outside of Auschwitz. From left to right they are: Josef Kramer, Anton Thumann, Karl Hocker and Franz Hossler. Hoessler was commandant of the women's camp in Auschwitz II (Birkenau). [Courtesy of USHMM ARCHIVES]

172. Time to relax from helping to instrument the last transports from Hungary, SS officer Karl Hocker takes his dog Favorit out on one of its regular walks outside the Auschwitz camp. [Courtesy of USHMM ARCHIVES]

173. Pictured on the far left is Josef Kramer (back to camera) and Dr Josef Mengele, Commandant Richard Baer and his adjutant Karl Hocker. Mengele went on to become the most highly decorated SS officer at Auschwitz to win the Iron Cross 1st Class. He had originally volunteered to come to Auschwitz in order to establish an experimental physiological and pathological department in the camp. He hadn't been in the camp very long before his sinister and merciless nature came to light. [Courtesy of USHMM ARCHIVES]

174. A group of SS officers stand in front of a building in Solahutte. Pictured facing the camera, second from the left is Karl Hocker. [Courtesy of USHMM ARCHIVES]

175. SS officers, including several SS physicians sit around a table drinking. Among those pictured are Karl Hocker (far left), Dr Fritz Klein (left hand side, end table), Dr Horst Schumann and Eduard Wirths on the right side of the bench, third from front. [Courtesy of USHMM ARCHIVES]

176. Two SS officers meet during the dedication of the new SS hospital in Auschwitz. Pictured on the left is Dr Enno Lolling and on the right is Dr Eduard Wirths. From September 1942 to January 1945, Wirth was the Chief SS doctor (SS-Standortarzt) at Auschwitz. He had formal responsibility for everything undertaken by the SS doctors (including Josef Mengele, Horst Schumann and Carl Clauberg) who worked in the medical sections of Auschwitz between 1942-1945. [Courtesy of USHMM ARCHIVES]

178. SS officer Oswald Pohl pays an official visit to Auschwitz. From the very start of its inception Pohl intended that Auschwitz would play a fundamental role in the concentration camp system in Upper Silesia and had high expectations of future economic success. [Courtesy of USHMM ARCHIVES]

179. SS officer Oswald Pohl pays an official visit to Auschwitz accompanied by Auschwitz Commandant Richard Baer who had previously served as his adjutant. [Courtesy of USHMM ARCHIVES]

180. Photograph taken in the summer of 1944 showing from left to right Richard Baer, Dr Josef Mengele, Josef Kramer, Rudolf Höss and an unidentified officer. [Courtesy of USHMM ARCHIVES]

181. During the summer of 1944 SS officers socialize at the SS retreat at Solahuette, near Auschwitz. From left to right Rudolf Höss, Josef Kramer, and an unidentified officer. [Courtesy of USHMM ARCHIVES]

182. Richard Baer, Dr Josef Mengele, and Rudolf Höss relax at the SS retreat at Solahuette during the summer of 1944. [Courtesy of USHMM ARCHIVES]

183. A group of SS officers gather in front of a building at Solahuette, the SS retreat outside of Auschwitz. From left to right are Josef Kramer, Dr Josef Mengele, Richard Baer, Karl Hocker and Walter Schmidetzki. [Courtesy of USHMM ARCHIVES]

184. At Auschwitz the SS held a number of comradeship meetings in order to try and encourage a sense of solidarity among the men. Although Höss had always found this type of solidarity a charade he nonetheless attended whenever he had time. Here in this photograph SS men sing along to the tune of an accordion at the SS retreat at Solahuette in the summer of 1944. Pictured in the front row are Karl Hoecker, Otto Moll, Rudolf Höss, Richard Baer, Josef Kramer (standing slightly behind Franz Hössler and partially obscured), Franz Hössler, and Josef Mengele. [Courtesy of USHMM ARCHIVES]

187. 188. 189. Three photographs showing SS officers gathering for shooting practise. On the far left is Karl Hocker. [Courtesy of USHMM ARCHIVES]

190.190a. Two photographs taken by a Russian photographic unit showing children that have survived Auschwitz. By their physical condition it is more than probable that they have not been in the camp very long. In one of the photographs they are asked to reveal their numbers tattooed on their left arm. [Courtesy of the Auschwitz-Birkenau Museum/USHMM - Yad Vashem Museum]

191. Two Russian soldiers help two women and a teenage boy through the quagmire of Birkenau during its liberation. On the afternoon of Saturday 27 January 1945, soldiers of the 60th Army of the First Ukrainian Front liberated Auschwitz. In total some 5,800 weak and undernourished prisoners in Birkenau were liberated. [Courtesy of the Auschwitz-Birkenau Museum]

192. Taken after the liberation of Auschwitz the photograph shows a half-naked dead women lying in the snow in January 1945. It is more than probable that she was one of many that were murdered prior to the evacuation of the camp. [Courtesy of the Auschwitz-Birkenau Museum]

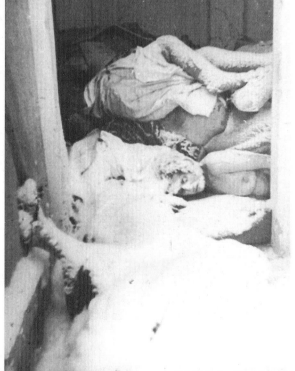

193. Piles of corpses inside the entrance of a wooden building after the liberation of the camp. On the night of 17 January 1945, some 58,000 prisoners were evacuated from Monowitz and the Auschwitz sub-camps; about 20,000 prisoners were evacuated from the Auschwitz-Birkenau camp alone. Special SS units that were left behind then proceeded to murder approximately 700 prisoners at Birkenau and nearby sub-camps. When news arrived that the Red Army were advancing along the main road from Krakow, the guards were ordered to destroy the remaining camp records, set fire to the Canada stores and exterminate the remaining prisoners. [Courtesy of the Auschwitz-Birkenau Museum]

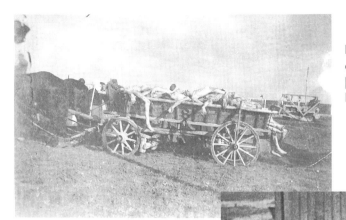

194. A cart full of corpses more than likely destined for either one of the crematoria or open air burning pits. [Courtesy of the Auschwitz-Birkenau Museum]

195. Half-naked malnourished corpses lay in the mud near one of the wooden barracks. They have been more than likely murdered by the SS prior to the evacuation of the camp in January 1945. [Courtesy of the Auschwitz-Birkenau Museum]

196. Many corpses have been found by Red Army troops still lying with blankets wrapped around their emaciated bodies. These hapless people have more than likely died of either malnutrition or disease. It's a grim reminder of what horror the Russian soldiers witnessed when they entered Auschwitz in January 1945. [Courtesy of the Auschwitz-Birkenau Museum]

197. Inmates well enough to sit up pose for the camera inside the Auschwitz hospital in January or February 1945. [Courtesy of the Auschwitz-Birkenau Museum]

198. On 25 May 1946, the former commandant of Auschwitz-Birkenau, Rudolf Höss, was finally handed over to the Polish authorities to face charges of war crimes against humanity. His trial started on 11 March 1947 lasting until 29 March 1947. He was found guilty of the murder of more than 2.5 million people at Auschwitz-Birkenau camp. However, this figure was later proven to be grossly inaccurate. [Courtesy of the Auschwitz-Birkenau Museum]

199. A Red Army officer converses with three Auschwitz prisoners standing next to a gibbet that was used frequently in Auschwitz. I to hang prisoners. [Courtesy of the Auschwitz-Birkenau Museum]

200.201. Two photographs showing the infamous railway line leading through the main gate of Birkenau. Completion of the railway line into the death camp was completed in the first half of May 1944, and used primarily for the transportation of Hungarian Jews to the camp. [Courtesy of the HITM ARCHIVE & Auschwitz-Birkenau Museum]

201b. From the main SS sentry observation post looking down the railway line to where Crematoria II (left) and Crematoria III (right) once stood. Right of the photograph is the area designated as B11, whilst to the left is the area known once as B1. [Courtesy of the HITM ARCHIVE & Auschwitz-Birkenau Museum]

201a. A photograph taken from the main entrance to the Auschwitz-Birkenau site. [Courtesy of the HITM ARCHIVE & Auschwitz-Birkenau Museum]

201c. From the main SS sentry observation post looking across to the left at Women's camp, designated as B1.a. [Courtesy of the HITM ARCHIVE & Auschwitz-Birkenau Museum]

202. From outside the main perimeter on the right is a barbed wire fence, and beyond that is a large area designated as BII-a,b,c,d,e, and f, which contained the Quarantine camp, Family camp for Theresienstadt Jews, camp for Hungarian Jews, Men's camp, Gypsy camp, and prisoner hospital area. [Courtesy of the HITM ARCHIVE & Auschwitz-Birkenau Museum]

203. A photograph taken from outside the main perimeter of Auschwitz-Birkenau in 2007 showing the outer camp fence and the wooden block stable barracks in the designated area known as BII. [Courtesy of the HITM ARCHIVE & Auschwitz-Birkenau Museum]

204. One of Auschwitz-Birkenau's prefabricated wooden guard towers along the perimeter fence of BII. [Courtesy of the HITM ARCHIVE & Auschwitz-Birkenau Museum]

205. A number of intact horse stable barracks at Auschwitz-Birkenau in BII-a, which was the designated area for the Quarantine camp. Note the drainage ditches. [Courtesy of the HITM ARCHIVE & Auschwitz-Birkenau Museum]

206. A photograph taken on the corner of the outer perimeter fence of BII-a looking down towards the camp's main entrance. [Courtesy of the HITM ARCHIVE & Auschwitz-Birkenau Museum]

207. The entrance to into the BII area of the camp. On the left was the former camp for Hungarian Jews, whilst on the right was the Men's camp. All the buildings in this area were blown-up by the SS when they evacuated the camp leaving just parts of the brick structure and chimney stacks intact. [Courtesy of the HITM ARCHIVE & Auschwitz-Birkenau Museum]

208. Showing part of the perimeter fence that separated the railway line and the area designated for Crematorium II. The brick buildings in the distance was in an area known as BI- b, which was part of the Women's camp. [Courtesy of the HITM ARCHIVE & Auschwitz-Birkenau Museum]

209. A photograph taken from inside BII looking across the camp's railway line to an area known as BI-a, which was part of the Women's camp. [Courtesy of the HITM ARCHIVE & Auschwitz-Birkenau Museum]

210. From the railway line the photograph shows part of the B1-b Women's camp with intact red brick barracks. The road between the railway line and the perimeter fence of the Women's camp led to Crematoria II and III. [Courtesy of the HITM ARCHIVE & Auschwitz-Birkenau Museum]

211.212. Two photographs showing the building known as the Central Sauna, which was completed by the autumn of 1943. It entered service in December 1943 and functioned as a disinfestation facility until January 1945. The building was situated at the far end of the camp behind the storage barracks of Canada. [Courtesy of the HITM ARCHIVE & Auschwitz-Birkenau Museum]

213. The camp's former water treatment facilities. This structure was situated between Crematorium III and the Canada storage facility at the far end of the camp. [Courtesy of the HITM ARCHIVE & Auschwitz-Birkenau Museum]

214. Concrete stairs leading down to the undressing chamber of Crematorium III. It was here where thousands of Jews descended these steps to undress prior to being gassed. [Courtesy of the HITM ARCHIVE & Auschwitz-Birkenau Museum]

215. Another view of the stairs leading down to the undressing chamber of Crematorium III. The undressing chamber measured 25ft in width and 169ft in length. A roof once covered the undressing chamber. [Courtesy of the HITM ARCHIVE & Auschwitz-Birkenau Museum]

216. Inside the undressing chamber of Crematorium III. The rubble is all that is left of the chamber's roof. [Courtesy of the HITM ARCHIVE & Auschwitz-Birkenau Museum]

217. The remains of Crematorium II. [Courtesy of the HITM ARCHIVE & Auschwitz-Birkenau Museum]

218. The remains of Crematorium V. According to a Czech prisoner the SS dynamited Crematorium V, which exploded about one o'clock in the morning on 26 January 1945, just twenty-four hours before the Red Army arrived. [Courtesy of the HITM ARCHIVE & Auschwitz-Birkenau Museum]

221. A typical red brick barracks inside the Women's camp B1-b. [Courtesy of the HITM ARCHIVE & Auschwitz-Birkenau Museum]

220. A photograph taken inside the Women's camp designated as B1-a. [Courtesy of the HITM ARCHIVE & Auschwitz-Birkenau Museum]

223. This wooden building was used by the notorious Josef Mengele. As camp physician Mengele had a never-ending supply of human specimens on whom to experiment. Wearing his white doctor's coat and gloves, he was usually present at the selection ramps in order to single out those unfit for work. Mengele was obsessed with genetics and the theory of a Nazi master race, and he availed of the selections to hand-pick victims for participation in his own sadistic medical trials. [Courtesy of the HITM ARCHIVE & Auschwitz-Birkenau Museum]

222. This is the inside of a building used for housing females in the Women's camp and clearly shows three bed wooden bunk system. [Courtesy of the HITM ARCHIVE & Auschwitz-Birkenau Museum]

225. A wooden guard tower on the outside of the perimeter fence of the Women's camp designated as B1-a. [Courtesy of Chandran Sivanason Aushwitz-Berkenau Museum]

226. The remains of the horse stable barracks in B11. The red brick chimneys and the flues are all that remain after the SS blew them up during the evacuation of the camp in January 1945. [Courtesy of Chandran Sivanason & Auschwitz-Birkenau Museum]